Votive plaque of Cleopatra as an Egyptian goddess.

The publishers would like to give particular thanks to Laurence Rees
and Ann Cattini of BBC *Timewatch*, and also Jonathan Lewis,
without whom this book would not have been possible.

THE SEARCH FOR CLEOPATRA

THE
SEARCH
FOR
CLEOPATRA

Michael Foss

Arcade Publishing • New York

FIRST U.S. EDITION

ISBN 1-55970-422-5
Library of Congress Catalog Card Number 97-74996
Library of Congress Cataloging-in-Publication information is available.

Published in the United States by Arcade Publishing, Inc., New York,
by arrangement with Michael O'Mara Books Limited, London
Distributed by Little, Brown and Company

10 9 8 7 6 5 4 3 2 1

Maps and artwork by Peter Funnell
Designed and typeset by Martin Bristow

PRINTED IN ENGLAND

CONTENTS

LIST OF MAPS

LIST OF
COLOUR PLATES

THE REIGNS OF THE PTOLEMIES 305–30 BC

Ptolemy I
Soter I
305–282 BC

Ptolemy VIII
Euergetes II
145–116 BC

Ptolemy II
Philadelphus
284–246 BC

Ptolemy IX
Soter II (Lathyrus)
115–107 BC

Ptolemy III
Euergetes I
246–222 BC

Ptolemy X
Alexander I
107–88 BC

Ptolemy IV
Philopator
222–205 BC

Ptolemy IX
Soter II (restored)
88–80 BC

Ptolemy V
Epiphanes
204–180 BC

Ptolemy XI
Alexander II
80 BC

Ptolemy VI
Philometor
180–145 BC

Ptolemy XII
Neus Dionysus (Auletes)
80–51 BC

Ptolemy VII
Neos Philopator
145 BC

Cleopatra VII
Philopator
51–30 BC

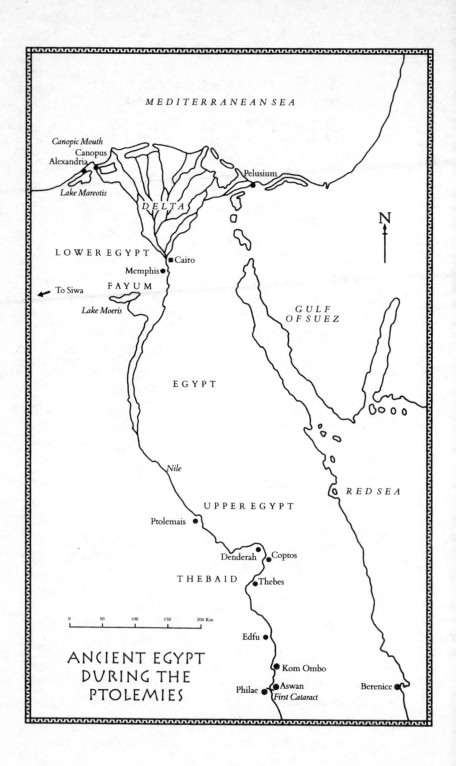

MEDITERRANEAN SEA

Canopic Mouth
Canopus
Alexandria
Pelusium
Lake Mareotis
DELTA

LOWER EGYPT
Cairo
Memphis
FAYUM
To Siwa
Lake Moeris

N

GULF
OF SUEZ

EGYPT

Nile

RED SEA

UPPER EGYPT

Ptolemais

Denderah Coptos

THEBAID Thebes

0   50   100   150   200 Km

Edfu

ANCIENT EGYPT
DURING THE
PTOLEMIES

Kom Ombo
Philae Aswan   Berenice
First Cataract

1

A SENSE
OF THE PAST

L ABORIOUS COLLECTIONS OF FACTS, gathered with ingenuity and great effort and judged with difficulty, make up our written histories. Out of this slow accumulation we build our picture of the past. But it is the picture not so much the evidence that we need, for our imagination seems to be primarily visual. And in our pictures what we most like – perhaps what we must have – is not some absolute of historical truth founded on a mountain of small certain facts. In any case, that is hardly possible, given the partial and much-erased record of history. Rather, we want a vision for the mind that reveals itself in drama, passion, elemental conflict, emblematic events that become the basis for mythologies.

Imagine a woman of sufficient interest to throw future ages into a labyrinth of dreams. Imagine her in all the variety and grace and appeal of mature womanhood taken to its utmost possibility, with the mind and a body to captivate a caesar, a world-conqueror, an emperor. Did such a person exist, or was she only a figment of the imagination?

History has suggested to us that there was such a woman, formed in the flesh and blood of an Egyptian queen of the

Alexander the Great arrived as the new conqueror of Egypt in
332 BC and so began the period when Egypt was ruled by the
Ptolemies from Macedonia on the Greek mainland.

first century BC. This woman – Cleopatra VII of the house of
Ptolemy – has appeared to later generations to contain all the
rare elements of a woman of dreams. She captivated not one
caesar but two, and made another one – the greatest of the
three – tremble so that one of his Romans wrote that Rome,
the city of conquerors, had feared only two people: Hannibal
and Cleopatra.

Who was this woman Cleopatra?

In June 323 BC, when Alexander the Great died suddenly in
Babylon after a short but meteoric life of conquest, his Macedonian generals scrambled for the remains of his empire. The
general Ptolemy, a tough and proven soldier who was also, in
the manner of so many men of the mountains, shrewd, obsti-
nate and wily, knew that he desired two things: the body of
Alexander and the land of Egypt.

For a man of good judgement these two objects of desire
went together; it was at the Egyptian oasis of Siwah that the
oracle of Amon had saluted Alexander as the son of the god.
Thus there began in Egypt the second and more remarkable
career of Alexander the Great, which turned him from a

successful conqueror – an ordinary piece of mortality – into a blazing star of mythology, a cult-hero and a god whose image became the possession of the world. Even today we see the embers of his fiery trail laid across the mind of humanity. A modern historian, following in the footsteps of Alexander, writes:

> We saw his story retold by Greek and Turkish shadow-players, and by Tadjik bards. We saw one of the last of the travelling one-man shows in Iran, complete with painted backdrop showing the death of the Persian king, Darius, in epic style. We heard about Greek medicine from the doctors of Multan in north-east Pakistan, who claim descent from Alexander's physicians; we sat in a felt yurt on the Turkmen steppe to hear the story of his devil's horns and his two-week sex romp with an Amazon queen.

Ptolemy wanted Egypt, the richest of all Alexander's conquests, and he knew that the possession of Alexander's corpse would give him the venerated body of a vivid new god and a talisman of extraordinary power in the ancient land. After discussions in Babylon, Ptolemy became satrap of Egypt, though there was doubt whether Alexander should be entombed at Siwah or in the Macedonian homeland at Aegae. Ptolemy hurried to take up his territory. Then while Perdiccas, the foremost of Alexander's generals, was engaged elsewhere, Ptolemy waylaid the funeral procession and took the hero's corpse to Memphis. Here, in the old capital of Lower Egypt, the body stayed until a fitting tomb – the Sema – was prepared in Alexander's own city of Alexandria. Within two years Perdiccas, who saw too late that he had been out-manoeuvred, attacked Egypt, but without success. In 321 BC he was stopped at the Nile. His invaders became the first of many enemies to the rule of the Ptolemies whose corpses were fed to the crocodiles of the river.

Now Ptolemy was securely confirmed as satrap of Egypt, and he had in his hands the body of the god Alexander and the god's magnificent new city of Alexandria. A state-cult was founded for Alexander, with its own priesthood. In 305 BC Ptolemy felt strong enough in his new land to transform himself from satrap to king. He took on the customary role of the pharaoh and assumed all the ancient rights and privileges of that great title. He became Ptolemy I Soter. Soter meant Saviour, and in taking that honorific title he claimed to be the man who had rescued Egypt from the hated rule of the Persians, he who had (as it was written in the hieroglyphics of a stele) restored to Horus, the god of Egypt, 'from this day forth forever, all its villages, all its towns, all its people, all its fields.'

In a hundred years or so of artful and successful rule, the first three Ptolemies had bound their family into a close-knit dynasty, and had bound that dynasty into the fabric and the being of Egypt. Quite consciously the house of Ptolemy kept the kingship confined within an incestuous family group. In a period of three hundred years two names alone sufficed for the successive kings. The male rulers were called Ptolemy, and sometimes, almost by way of an aside to bring forth great memories, also Alexander. Their co-rulers, the powerful and ruthless queens of the dynasty, were called Berenice or Arsinoe or Cleopatra – nothing else. The kings advertised themselves to their people with such titles as Soter (Saviour) and Euergetes (Benefactor) and Epiphanes (Shown-by-God). They and their queens were called Philadelphus (Brother or Sister-loving) or Philopator (Father-loving) or Philometor

Founder of the Ptolemy dynasty, Ptolemy I Soter (305–282 BC)
had been one of Alexander the Great's best generals
before becoming ruler of Egypt.

(Mother-loving). These titles were too often more than
rhetoric, indicating a real marriage between brother and sister
or between parent and child. This habit of incest, for which
there was perhaps some slight precedent in Egyptian history,
scandalized the Greeks. But the Ptolemies, those pragmatic
ruffians from the highlands of Macedonia, though Greek-
speaking and of Greek culture themselves, saw only a dynastic
advantage in incest. They were far from their homeland and
their regal actions were not subject to review from their
Greek peers.

In three centuries of intermittent in-breeding there is no
clear evidence that the family degenerated excessively as a
result. The Ptolemy men ran to fat. They lost the hardiness
and mental toughness of pasturalists from the hills, and the
later kings became idle, artistic and a little decadent. But that
is a familiar course in realms that have become rich, lazy and

somnolent. The Ptolemy queens, on the contrary, remained sharp-witted, competent and energetic. However, it is possible that Cleopatra VII, the most brilliant of those queens, gained some of her exceptional qualities from an infusion of new blood. The identity of neither her mother nor her grand-mother is known for certain. On the maternal side, she sprang from concubines rather than queens.

It was a bold step to root the family inheritance on incest. But it was a move of greater wisdom, carefully carried through by the first three Ptolemy kings, to assimilate as much as pos-sible the government by this alien Macedonian Greek ruling house into the long-standing, stable traditions of Egyptian life and practice.

In the ancient world Greeks and Egyptians were no strangers to each other. Both were seafaring people. Trade and culture had been intermixed between them for a long time. The histories of Herodotus, from the fifth century BC, showed how much was known about Egypt, and with what keen intellectual curiosity (the mark of ancient Greece!) the Greeks investigated all aspects of the civilization of the colos-sus of the Near East. Among many wonders, two things were easy to note: the longevity and resilience of pharaonic civiliza-tion; and the wealth and productive power of the land, owed in large part to the gifts of the Nile. And shrewd minds – there was no shortage of those among Greeks – also saw that the two things were closely connected.

The wealth of Egypt was obvious. Time and again, when the prodigal Nile had performed its yearly miracle of flood and soil-enrichment, the price of Egyptian wheat in the Athenian market was able to undercut the price of the local produce, despite transportation costs and a middleman's profit. Wheat and barley were the staples of Egyptian agriculture, which produced in good years a large surplus for export. But the fine silt of the Nile under a warm sun was capable of supporting almost any harvest, and the variety of things grown in Egypt with success was extraordinary. Vines, olives, figs, dates, walnuts, beans, peas, lentils, cabbage, radish, onions and garlic, all did very well. Spices included mustard, cumin and fenugreek. Oil was pressed from linseed, safflower, sesame and croton. There were nuts of many kinds, and the fruits of a warm climate such as apricots, peaches and quinces. From the stock of barley, large amounts of beer were brewed and thankfully drunk on hot harvest days.

Nor was there a shortage of pasturage for the animals. Draught oxen did the heavy work, ploughing the shallow furrow or turning the waterwheels of the irrigation system on which the success of agriculture depended. On large estates, in the south and at the desert edge, camels were used, as awkward and bad-tempered here as elsewhere. 'You can hear from your brother', a letter-writer complains, 'how everyone here suffered on account of those camels from Coptos.' Bulls had a special place in a society that held them to be sacred. They, too, were not easy to handle. 'Those damn bulls of yours', runs the same letter, 'are running wild, and they've landed me in court several times, thanks to you.' Ubiquitous donkeys carried the peasants and the lighter loads. The housewife was likely to have her chickens and a dovecote. Pigs snuffled in courtyards (the Greeks were fond of pork and bacon but the animal was unclean to the Egyptians). Sheep and goats in large numbers gave meat and wool and milk and cheese.

The bulk of the produce, certainly the surplus for export, came from the large estates of the king, the nobles and the temple priesthood, in the Nile delta or in the Fayum where the early Ptolemies drained part of Lake Moeris, to extend the good land on which they could settle their Greek followers or reward mercenary soldiers with landholdings. But the pattern of production and commerce developed in Egypt over several millennia was complex and varied, and the aim of the Ptolemies was not to change it but to refine it and develop it further. Production extended well beyond the dominating great estates whose prime purpose was to enrich the king. The sub-lessee, the smallholder, the cultivator of a domestic plot, the entrepreneur, the official with a sideline in agriculture and business, all played an important part in the accumulation of Egyptian wealth. So long as the main current of labour flowed to the king – to the state – it was permissible that some of the flow should run into the winding channels of individual enterprise.

Beyond all systems of landholding and production lay the annual problem of the Nile. The success or failure of almost all agriculture depended on the control and distribution of the river-waters – on the rise and fall of the river. In June, the waters began to swell around the First Cataract in the far south. The flood proceeded down the river to the delta, and then began slowly to fall, starting in September. On this simple rhythm the life of the country depended. 'When two sources of the Nile have been closed up,' said an ancient inscription, 'plants will wither and life will retreat from the living.' Anxiously, the river was watched and measured, with large scales cut into the stone at various points on the bank. The readings were collected and collated, for the balance between dearth and plenty was very fine, as a Roman historian observed:

Seven metres is an average rise. Less does not irrigate all the available land, and more holds back the sowing by too much wetness; with less the soil is parched, with more it is water-logged. Each district takes a careful note of both extremes. In a rise of five and a half metres one sees the spectre of famine, and even in six metres hunger is felt. But six and a half metres brings good cheer, six and threequarters confidence, and seven metres delight. The largest rise to date was eight metres, and the smallest a little over two metres, in the year of Pharsalus, as if the river by portents was trying to warn of the murder of Pompey.

The yearly drama of the vast river, stretching some thousand kilometres from the First Cataract to the sea, only unfolded slowly. Different parts of the land were affected at different times. To control the water and make it work for the benefit of the whole land needed a co-ordinated effort to plan and measure and inform, to build and maintain canals, dykes and ditches, to work waterwheels and sluices, to dam or to let flow. All this required central direction, a large bureaucracy of administrators, and a large workforce to be deployed at will under the king, who in the theory of the state was the only autocratic authority that the country possessed. Whether the centralized bureaucracy and planned economy of Egypt grew out of the people's need to control the river, or whether the control of the Nile resulted from the already established forms of pharaonic society, is a question shrouded by its antiquity. But the plain fact was that the system worked. It took no great intelligence to see its success in the long waving green of the cornfields, in vineyards and olive groves, in stands of date palms, in the grape-hung trellises of country houses, in the orchards of ripe fruit. Men saw it even more in the grain warehouses waiting to discharge their surplus into the ships of all the Mediterranean, in the pomp of palaces, and in temples and monuments that dwarfed the scale of all other man-made objects. They knew that this was success.

In the early years of his reign, Ptolemy I Soter saw that the impressive bureaucratic structure in Egypt had suffered under the maladministration of the Persians. The river system had been neglected and agriculture was in decline. Trade was in the hands of foreigners, mainly Greeks and Phoenicians. Industry was hardly maintained, except by the priests of the temples. Power was shifting away from the kingship into the temple complexes. Ptolemy I, and more particularly his son Ptolemy II Philadelphus, set out to re-establish and re-interpret the old autocratic system even more stringently than before, enforcing bureaucratic efficiency with military severity.

The Ptolemaic king [a leading historian has written] has to be thought of as a landowner and a farmer on a huge scale, one whose estate was the whole land of Egypt. All the officials were his personal servants, the army an instrument of his will, raised from the men who had plots of land assigned to them out of his territory on the condition of rendering him military service.

Ptolemy I was a soldier and his experience of men and affairs came from the campaign of Alexander; under the first Ptolemaic kings 'there was no sharp distinction between the military and the civil career, and the staff of the king bore an almost purely military character'.

The king was the ultimate beneficiary of all activity of whatever kind within the state. For the early Ptolemies, the boast of Louis XIV of France was nothing but the truth: 'The State, it is me.' The whole land was plotted and divided into

[18]

The Ptolemies re-established the old Egyptian custom of
royal brother and sister marriages and Arsinoe II, seen here
depicted as a goddess, was married to her brother, Ptolemy II.

highly regulated administrative districts, and administration
was in the hands of a large centralized bureaucracy whose
chief officers, usually eunuchs, were royal placeholders. The
underlying principle of all government was the enrichment of
the king. And though the ruler naturally delegated his authority, the people did not forget that the authority was his, nor
did they hesitate to remind him that the ultimate responsibility was his also. A conscientious Ptolemy was a busy man. He
was bombarded with petitions from even the meanest of his
subjects. An historian, leafing through the evidence of the
papyri, noted the following causes of complaint:

Someone has killed the pigs of an allotment holder; a
provision merchant has made a fraudulent delivery; joint
tenants are squabbling about the partition of a field; a careless

attendant has scalded a woman in a public bath house; a prostitute spat on a man when he turned her offer down.

All this was presented to the king for adjudication, and a myriad of other things had to be looked into as well. Quite typically, in 99 BC the chief embalmer of the divine bulls Apis and Mnevis finds the insolence of officialdom too much to bear. He writes to the king, demanding a royal command, to be pinned on his door, that he should be left alone. The command is duly prepared and signed and sent. No wonder a good king was a weary man. It was said that one of the Seleucid monarchs, who operated in Syria a similar but less grandiose system, cried out in distress. 'If only the people knew', he lamented, 'what weary work it is to write and read so many letters, they would not even bother to pick up a diadem from the ground.' But the efficient running of the Ptolemaic state, both in theory and practice, demanded the constant care of the king.

If the king was overwhelmed by work, his subjects were, on the face of it, oppressed by taxes, regulations and lack of freedom. 'No one', declared a Ptolemaic decree, 'has the right to do what he wishes, but everything is organized for the best.' The state had in its armoury a powerful battery of taxes, imposts, dues, duties and tolls that bore on all production, industry, commerce, international trade, and all contractual relations. The state also had judicial and coercive powers to enforce the multitudinous regulations. These officials collected taxes on professions and handicrafts, on manufacture and distribution, on sales, on building, on livestock and on slaves, on the use of bath houses, on the navigation of canals, and on the crossing of bridges. Many important commodities were royal monopolies, safeguarded by a heavy duty on imports. Oil, wool, figs, honey, beer and venison, among other things, were protected in this way. Banking and coinage were solely in the hands of the state. The economy became fully monetarized, in contrast to payment in kind under the pharaohs, though poor cultivators would still give up part of their produce in place of land tax.

Without doubt, the hand of bureaucracy held the people in a hard, oppressive grip. But when the system worked well it not only enriched the king but also raised the general level of prosperity, extending down even to the lowest *fellahin*. There is evidence, too, that within the intricacy of the regulations there was leeway for small personal ventures, for private initiatives and individual enterprise. Nor was the system rigidly inhumane, for the king knew that his own security and wealth depended on the well-being of the whole country. The wiser Ptolemies were quite ready, in hard times, to lessen burdens, remit taxes, and cancel traditional obligations.

Rostovtzeff, the great Russian historian to whom we owe so much of our knowledge of the period, thought that this excessively centralized state made a dreary picture, and led to no advance in the happiness of the people. But it has been pointed out that, in the economy, the Ptolemaic rule in Egypt was a great advance, if not in freedom and happiness (but what did any peasant or labourer in the ancient world know of those fine ideals?), then at least in the briskness of production and trade, and the corresponding accumulation of wealth, throughout the land.

Together with a strong economy went, finally, a settled foreign and military policy. Naturally, there were still many wars. In the crumbling of Alexander's empire, the detritus of war spread all over eastern lands as far as India. And the crises remained, for the princes of the time had not given up opportunism, jealousy, pride, greed or dynastic ambition. But in Egypt, just as the land rested crucially on the gifts of the Nile, so the early Ptolemies saw that the security of the realm depended on a compact and adequate defence of the great river valley. Campaigns beyond that, to influence trade routes through Arabia or to gain territory to the north and east of Syria, were a risk and an adventure.

From the barrens of the south and the desert of the west there was no great danger. Upper Egypt, the southern third of the country known as the Thebaid, followed a sunny, traditional semi-autonomous way of life not much checked by the Greek officials of Alexandria. The Red Sea town of Berenice, far to the south, watched over the eastern sea-route and kept an eye on the valuable emerald mines nearby. Otherwise, the wilderness of sand and scrub and heat was protection enough against primitive tribes. But in the northeast and north there was much more danger. The usual path of invasion into Egypt lay to the north of the Red Sea, in the relatively short westward march from Palestine across the desert to the Nile delta. This was the area that all rulers of Egypt guarded closely, with the main garrison at Pelusium on the most easterly of the delta river-mouths. This historical danger from the north-east caused the Ptolemies to watch Syria anxiously. They would meddle there as far as they could, in particular trying to keep control, either by conquest or through a client-king, of Coele-Syria, the territory better known as Palestine.

The other danger from the north was likely to come from naval attack in the eastern Mediterranean. To counteract this threat, the Ptolemies pushed into the North African coastal lands of Cyrene, to the west of Egypt, and took control of Cyprus, the dominating island at the east end of the inland sea. They also kept up the naval power of Egypt, which was traditionally strong, encouraging ship-building, maintaining a large fleet and protecting it in Alexandria with the best and most extensive harbour system in the Mediterranean. A foothold in Palestine and Cyprus also provided timber for the ship-builders, for Egypt, though it was lavish with many things, was very short of trees.

In their plan for Egypt the early Ptolemies made a success of practical matters. They were helped by careful observation and good sense, and they had the good fortune to combine Greek intelligence with the hard-headed ruthlessness of seasoned Macedonian campaigners. It was perhaps more surprising that they quickly saw, or intuited, the fundamental place of religion in the structure of Egyptian society. Of course, no man could miss the temples, the statues, the pyramids and the monuments of the past. But to understand Egyptian religious sensibility was a difficult task, yet the rulers of the house of Ptolemy managed to reconcile their lives and their government with the feeling and the forms of Egyptian religion.

The religion they found was not new to the Greeks. Much about the Egyptian gods had been discovered already by traders and travellers, and on the whole the Greeks had been impressed by the antiquity, the solemnity and the splendour of the religion. Certain Greek gods became roughly identified with Egyptian gods, though Greeks, and more so Romans, found a crocodile-god or one with the head of a hawk puzzling and a little distasteful. This was despite such imaginings of hellenism as the goat-legged Pan, or the centaurs who were half horse and half man.

But both peoples thought about religion in much the same way. Neither had any notion of a transcendental theology. No one in the ancient world but the Israelites had come to terms with that idea. Egyptians as well as Greeks needed mythological stories to explain to themselves features of a universe that seemed almost wholly mysterious. Within these stories, the gods were figures-in-action who licensed the processes of the world, processes whose causative principles were in general unknown. The gods took on human form because mankind knew no higher or more noble form to copy. And sometimes they took on the forms of beasts because certain animals were dangerous or beautiful or helpful, and danger, beauty and helpfulness were attributes worthy of a god. A large part of ancient religion was a placatory ritual, a form of good manners towards the unknown.

But Egypt, autocratic by long history and bureaucratic by design, more than most other lands had made religion an integral part of state life. The temples and the priesthood had traditionally played an important role in the economy and the administration of large estates. The evidence of religion was always present in the eyes of the people. It was put to use in a thorough and practical way, and the gods were familiar beings. The great ones – Amon, Isis, Osiris, Horus, Hathor, Thoth – were honoured in great temples with all that money, labour and imagination could provide. But a small town on the edge of the Fayum, in the second century of Ptolemaic rule, had room for 13 little temples or shrines to gods both great and small. And temple precincts, besides being homes for the gods, were also social and economic centres of activity. The greater precincts might include factories for linen making, papyrus works, mills, breweries, brickworks and stone yards. Vendors, traders, hawkers and hustlers used the precinct as a marketplace. And a discreet brothel often helped to swell the temple coffers.

In Egypt, since everything sensible to mankind was capable of being a part of divinity, there was nothing incongruous in divine kingship. The gods had no hierarchy, nor were they uniform throughout the country. Local enthusiasm championed local gods. So a god-king, in theory equally present and visible to all his people, gave unity to religion, just as the pharaoh's absolute supremacy in civil society gave unity to the state. The pharaohs had been gods; Alexander had been proclaimed one by the oracle of Amon. When the early Ptolemies joined the inheritance of Alexander with the traditions of Egypt, they saw no reason why they should not be gods too; and there were many good practical reasons to encourage the people to accept them as such. Ptolemy I had been acclaimed, and perhaps worshipped, as Saviour. His son Ptolemy II took a step logical to Egyptians when he declared the divinity of his own parents (Theocritus said he was the first Greek ever to do so), and from this position his own divinity was only a few paces down the same road.

In 278 BC the festival of the Ptolemaeia was instituted in Alexandria in honour of the deified Ptolemy Soter. Every four years the festival took place amid the games, processions and feasts that the Greek-speaking Alexandrians loved so much. For although this was a feast of the Egyptian religious calendar, it bore every mark of its Greek inspiration.

> The whole pomp has a non-Egyptian air [wrote an old authority]. If we except the curious products of Nubia and Ethiopia in ivory, giraffes, antelopes, hippopotami, etc., there is nothing Egyptian in the whole affair. We seem to see a Hellenistic king spending millions on a Hellenistic feast.

But that was the way with much religion in the ancient world. It was inclusive and syncretic. A new god was not rejected for alien birth or unusual ways. Egyptians had a place in their

[25]

devotions for a god who spoke and looked and acted like a Greek.

This was just what the ruling house desired. The Ptolemies worked hard to ensure the acceptance of their deified kings throughout all their realm. In 238 BC, in the reign of Ptolemy III Euergetes, a proclamation from Canopus in the Nile delta was inscribed in hieroglyphic, demotic and Greek, to be promulgated in all temples down to those of the third rank:

> Let it be resolved by the priests in all the land to increase the honour and awe that already exist in the temples for King Ptolemy and Queen Berenice, the Benefactor Gods, and to their parents, the Brother-and-Sister Gods, and to their grandparents, the Saviour Gods; and let it be resolved that the priests in all the temples in all the land should be called in all documents priests of the Benefactor Gods, and that this should be engraved on the rings they wear.

To the four existing tribes of the Egyptian priesthood, a fifth tribe was added devoted to the service of the Benefactor Gods. Their feast was to be celebrated each year 'on the day when the star of Isis rises, which is the day of the new year in the holy records'.

Egyptian gods had been identified with Greek opposites – Hathor and Aphrodite, for example, or Amon and Zeus – and Ptolemaic god-kings had been added to the Egyptian pantheon. But nothing indicated the cheerful invention of ancient religious sensibility better than the cult of Sarapis, a hugely popular synthesis that combined the reverence given to the dead and mummified bulls of Apis, entombed at Memphis, with the traditional worship of Osiris, god of the dead. In Alexandria, and particularly at the Serapeum in Memphis,

the new cult, a Greek inspiration despite its Egyptian dress-
ing, received numberless petitions and prayers from its devo-
tees. The oldest surviving papyrus in Greek records the
curses of a certain Artemisia, a Greek woman, who calls on
'Lord Oserapis' to avenge her against the brute who made
her pregnant.

Formally, in the marrying together of old and new institutions and in their interpretation of society, the Ptolemies had
adapted excellently to the traditions and practices of Egypt.
From the lofty view of the court at Alexandria, taken over a
period of almost three hundred years, the Ptolemaic kings had
preserved the integrity, stability and prosperity of the country.
The best efforts of their administration had been industrious
and conscientious, in touch with everyday needs and popular
psychology.

> During your tour of inspection [ran a typical official instruc-
> tion from the middle Ptolemaic period] as you go about try to
> encourage everyone and make them feel happier, and not by
> word only. If there are complaints against the scribes or the
> village chieftains, about the fields or the harvests, look into
> the matter and try to put it right immediately.

But down on the ground, where the Egyptian *fellahin*
rubbed against the Greek official, townsman or settler, the
limited evidence seems to show that there was little meeting
of minds and little common interest. To the native Egyptians,
the Greeks were the masters who imposed upon their lives.
These impositions were perhaps no more burdensome than
before, under their own pharaohs, but the ordinary people
noted that the traffic of respect, privilege and authority tended
to go one way only, in a direction favourable to the Greeks.

Greeks preferred to live in their towns – Ptolemais or their resplendent capital of Alexandria – or on the rich lands of the north, in the estates of the delta or the Fayum. The further one went from Lower Egypt towards the baked lands of the Thebaid, the more tenuous was the Greek presence and the more stubborn the survival of ancient practices. There was a suspicion between the old stock and the newcomers with their attendant flock of aliens, mercenaries and adventurers. It grated on the Egyptians that they were the ones who were expected to change, to learn Greek, to take Greek names, to ape the ways of foreigners. 'They have treated me with contempt', a native camel owner complained, 'because they think I'm a barbarian. I do not know how to behave like a Greek.' The Egyptians could not help but notice how strongly the Greeks clung to their superior status and their privileges, specially in the law-courts.

Yet the Greeks for their part were often shocked by the unshifting conservatism of the Egyptians, their plodding refusal to leave the well-worn ancestral tracks, and their indifference to the fresh adventure (as the Greeks saw it) of hellenistic culture and thought. 'Some of them had stones and sticks in their hands', wrote a functionary of the Serapeum at Memphis, complaining of an attack on him by the temple cleaners, 'and wanted to put me to death because I am a Greek.'

The two peoples met together in the press of daily life, and they inter-married often enough. They made small accommodations in their lives, and put up with each other for pragmatic reasons, not because they were in sympathy, even after many generations of living side by side. A mutual understanding was hard to achieve. The kings, as a matter of policy, built, repaired or embellished many temples, at Karnak, Philae,

The Ptolemaic rulers built, repaired or embellished many
of the ancient Egyptian temples, including Karnak,
the largest religious centre in Egypt.

Edfu, Denderah, Kom Ombo and on several lesser sites. But
when the two peoples prayed to a god vaguely identified as
Amon Zeus, the Egyptian idea of Amon was very different
from the Greek conception of Zeus. What the Egyptians saw
in their religion was the history of their imagination; what the
Greeks liked it in was the age-old appeal to superstition, to
oracles, spells, curses, horoscopes, talismans, amulets and
mysterious occult practices. When a Greek wanted a dream
interpreted, or a potion to help him in love or against illness,
he was likely to go to an Egyptian.

We have a picture, therefore, of Ptolemaic Egypt that
shows an imposing, substantial edifice built on the foundations of some three thousand years of Egyptian history, newly

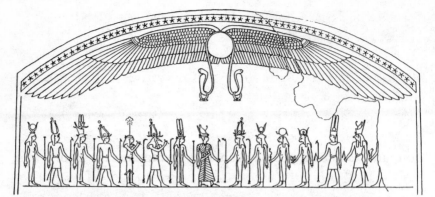

The Kom el-Hisn stela depicts a display of regal worship by the early Ptolemies. Ptolemy II and his wife, Berenice II, are standing facing a procession of gods (right) while being followed by Thoth, Seschat and the deified kings Ptolemy II, Arsinoe II and Ptolemy I.

enlivened and decorated by Greek political good sense and intellectual achievement. But a closer look reveals a worrying subsidence in the foundations, a lack of cohesion in the structure, evidence everywhere of cracks and weakness. For the Greeks, the grandeur of the conception was still attractive, and there were sufficient advantages to draw them and other foreigners to the country in great numbers. For adventurers and young men of spirit Ptolemaic Egypt was the place to be. They poured in, looking for excitement and good times, as the poet Herodas pictured them in one of his entertainments:

Egypt! Everything that is, or can be anywhere, is in Egypt. Riches, power, comfort, glory, shows, games, gymnasiums, young men, gold, philosophers, the shrine of the Brotherand-Sister Gods, the king (a liberal sort of fellow), the Museum, wine – all the good things a young man's heart can possibly desire. Yes, and women too, more numerous than the

stars, and as beautiful as the goddesses that submitted themselves to the Judgment of Paris.

On the evidence of the Greeks, the house of Ptolemy had
good reason for satisfaction.

But for the Egyptians, as they were fretted by the growing
incompetence of a complicated, over-centralized administration, and as decadence weakened the king and the court, and
corruption polluted the bureaucracy, a sullen dissatisfaction
became more widespread. Small revolts broke out from time
to time, particularly in the far south of Upper Egypt, many of
them encouraged by the Egyptian priesthood of the temple of
Amon-Ra at Thebes. And in the outside world Roman eyes
began to calculate the weakness of the later Ptolemies, covet-
ing the wealth of the land.

The wealth was still there, for accumulation had become a
habit like everything else. But by the turn of the first century
BC fatigue had set in. There was a presentment of this weari-
ness even in the successful reign of Ptolemy II Philadelphus. It
was said that as he, a plump man of sixty-three with gout,
came close to the time of his death in 245 BC, he saw from the
window of his palace in Alexandria a group of poor Egyptian
labourers lying on the canal bank, at ease on the warm sand,
eating with contentment the few scraps of their midday food.
Then he cried out bitterly against the tedious effort of his
royal lot and wished himself with no more burdens than those
of his simplest subject.

2

PREPARATION OF A QUEEN

T HE GROSS MAN in the robes of diaphanous gauze, who
was called Physkon (Fatty) by the caustic tongue of the
Alexandrian mob, on the death of his brother in Syria at last
secured the throne of Egypt in 145 BC. As a gesture of hope he
took the title Ptolemy VIII Euergetes II, attempting to raise
the memory of the first great Ptolemy Euergetes, when the
flush of success was on Egypt. The attempt was useless. The
house of Ptolemy was in decline, and the kings of the second
century BC struggled to hold their state together. In his boy-
hood Ptolemy Physkon had seen Antiochus, the Seleucid king
of Syria, acting the pharaoh in Memphis itself. Physkon's
brother, Ptolemy VI, another fat man, had reclaimed some of
the reputation and power of Egypt, handsomely defeating the
Syrians just before he died of a battle-wound. In fact, in the
way of the ancient world, his doctors had killed him, making
fatal a head-wound that he might well have survived. This
Ptolemy VI, said the historian Polybius, was a competent
man, brave and decisive in battle, but when there was no crisis
he became slack, idle and pleasure-loving, all of which was

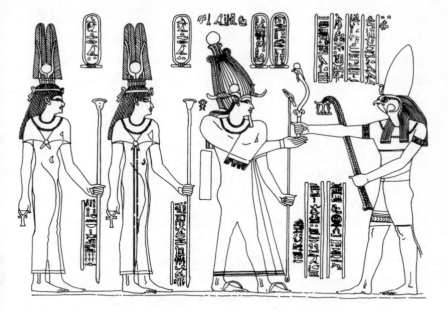

Sandstone relief, *c.* 135 BC, from Kom Ombo temple showing
Ptolemy VIII Euergetes II receiving a scimitar from Haroeris or
Horus the Elder, the falcon god. Behind him are Ptolemy's
wives, Cleopatra II and Cleopatra III.

'rather Egyptian'. That succinct judgement was an epitome of
the Ptolemaic failure.

In the deadly intrigues of the family, Physkon had schemed
hard for the crown, and he did not intend to let go of his
advantage. His brother, the late king, had left a little son
already associated, in the way of the ruling house, with the
kingship of his father. Physkon settled that small matter by
having his nephew – Ptolemy VII – murdered 'in the arms of
his mother', as the hostile rumours reported. Again according
to custom, Physkon then married that same mother, Cleopatra II, who was his own sister and also the widow of his dead
brother. This Cleopatra, in the previous reign, had been

Physkon's grim enemy, and in this she had been supported by the Jews of Alexandria. One of the first acts of the new king had been to turn his elephants loose in the Jewish quarter, hoping to trample the inhabitants to death. The Jews, wrote Josephus, were saved by the natural delicacy of the elephants and by the intervention of the king's concubine Irene.

After a year of consolidation against his many enemies, Ptolemy Physkon was crowned and at about the same time Cleopatra II gave birth to his child. The feast in honour of this baby prince was marred by the slaughter of some citizens from Cyrene who had made rude remarks about the mistress Irene. Within a short time of this birth, Physkon lost patience with his sister-wife and transferred his sexual attention to his niece, the teenage daughter of his queen by her dead husband-brother. It was said that Physkon raped this girl; then he married her bigamously under the title Cleopatra III. From this time, about the year 140 BC, there were three sovereigns in Egypt. The official documents referred to the elder queen as 'Cleopatra the Sister' and to the younger one as 'Cleopatra the Wife'.

The older woman could not be put away because she was, as so often with the queens of the Ptolemies, a forceful, astute politician with a strong following in the country. The rift in the royal family symbolized the breaks and disintegration within society, particularly in Alexandria. Cabals formed, armed partisans took sides, the fickle mob bayed out its passion. In 130 BC, after 10 years of bitterness, the mob burned down the king's palace in Alexandria, and Physkon fled to Cyprus with his children and his young queen Cleopatra III.

Cruelty, selfishness, rebellion, sexual confusion – Alexandria was the cockpit where these humours bred and multiplied. Visitors agreed that the city was a place apart from the kingdom. It was the Ptolemaic capital, but it was not Egypt.

Bronze drachma piece with a representation of the great Pharos
lighthouse which was designed by the architect Sostratus
in the reign of Ptolemy II.

And as long as the kings were tempted to plot and play and
parade in Alexandria, they withdrew from responsibility and
endangered the government of their Egyptian lands.

There was no city like it in the West or in all the kingdoms
as far as India. Founded by Alexander the Great in 331 BC, it
bore his illustrious name, and its fame matched his own. It
began with a small Egyptian village called Rhakotis, on a
slight elevation of good land between a lake and the sea. Here,
the architect Dinocrates of Rhodes was given a free hand to
plan a city that would marry Greek rationality with Greek
magnificence. To the south, the site was guarded by the wide
waters of Lake Mareotis. The Mediterranean shore-line was
protected by the long offshore island of Pharos and a reef. A
short distance to the east the Canopic mouth of the Nile emptied into the sea; and in the west the desert edged in towards
the city limit. In this favourable place there rose in time an
orderly oblong grid of streets and buildings, 6 kilometres on
its longer side, which fully realized the inspiration of the
architects. The geographer Strabo, who visited the city
shortly after the death of Cleopatra, admired what he saw:

The whole city is crossed by streets wide enough for horses and carriages, and intersecting at right angles are two very wide streets, being more than 30 metres in breadth. The city has magnificent public places and buildings and royal palaces that cover a quarter, even a third, of the total city area. Each king, just as he adds ornaments to public buildings, also builds a palace of his own to join those already there. And all are connected to the harbour, even those beyond the harbour walls. Also forming part of the palace quarter is the Sema, the enclosure containing the tomb of Alexander and those of the kings . . . In a word, the city is full of dedications and sanctuaries. The gymnasium is the most beautiful building, with a colonnade about 175 metres in length. In the middle of the city are the law courts and open groves. There is also the Paneum, an artificial conical hill with spiral steps going round it. From the top, the whole wonderful city spreads out below.

Joining the island of Pharos to the mainland was a causeway of more than a thousand pieces, called the Heptastadion. This divided the inshore waters into two harbours. To the east was the Great Harbour into which ships were guided by the gigantic Pharos lighthouse, one of the wonders of the world. The palace complex, the Brucheion, a city within a city, adjoined this harbour and had its own protected anchorage. To the west was the larger and more open Eunostos, the Harbour of Happy Return.

The hallmarks of the city were clarity, order, practicality and magnificence. Spaciously laid out, tightly regulated, decorated with taste and expense, Alexandria expressed the logical and artistic possibilities of the Greek mind. For the citizens, it was intended to be the setting for fulfilled lives that took into account the needs of the whole person, spirit, body and mind.

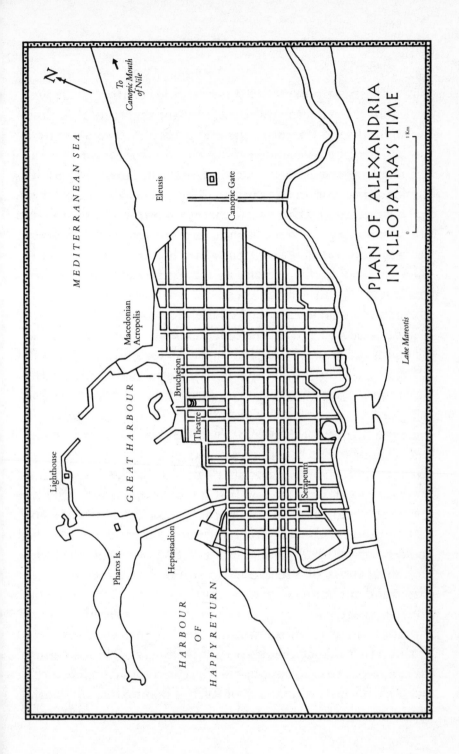

PLAN OF ALEXANDRIA
IN CLEOPATRA'S TIME

MEDITERRANEAN SEA

To
Canopic Mouth
of Nile

Eleusis

Canopic Gate

Macedonian
Acropolis

Lighthouse

GREAT HARBOUR

Brucheion

Theatre

Pharos Is.

Heptastadion

Serapeum

HARBOUR
OF
HAPPY RETURN

Lake Mareotis

0   1 Km

The majesty of power and the awe of kingship were represented in the palaces and the public architecture. Religious
sensibility found a home in the many temples, in the tombs of
the Sema where Alexander and the god-kings of the dynasty
rested, and particularly in the Serapeum, the shrine of Sarapis,
the favourite god of Alexandria. The body was fed, clothed
and entertained by the wealth that flowed from the vast trade
of the capital, which was also the largest port of the Mediterranean. The mind was nurtured within the gymnasium (a
place for both bodily exercise and mental instruction), and by
the learning and artistic creativity that poured out of the
Museum, to which was attached the great Library.

The Museum – the house dedicated to the Muses – was
based on the ancient practice of the philosophical schools in
Athens. In time, under the sympathetic patronage of the
Ptolemies, it became the powerhouse of western learning and
the glory of the city. It was housed in stately buildings within
the royal quarter of Brucheion, with its director appointed by
and responsible to the king. The poets Callimachus, Apollonius of Rhodes and Theocritus worked for the Museum. It
produced good literature and better scholarship. In the Library
that formed part of the Museum there was a collection of some
half a million rolls and parchments and papyri. Here was the
greater part of the thought and the writing of the Greek world,
including most of the Homeric works, gathered, lovingly
edited and annotated and, most important of all, preserved for
future ages. All this was a credit to the Ptolemaic kings, men
with many human faults but with sound artistic impulses.

Literature and scholarship were well-served, but the most
valuable work to come out of the Museum was that done in science. Without Callimachus or even Theorcritus, the world
would have suffered a slight loss. Without the invention and

View of the city of Alexandria from a sixteenth-century book of
engravings, the *Liber Chronicarum* by H Schedel. Founded by
Alexander the Great, the city became one of the most magnificent
in the eastern Mediterranean during the Ptolemaic dynasty
and was renowned for its culture.

discoveries of Euclid and others in mathematics, of Archimedes
and later Hero in theoretical and applied physics, of Eratosthenes and Claudius Ptolemy in geography, of Eratosthenes
again and Aristarchus in astronomy and calendar reform, and
finally of Erasistratus in medicine, what would have become of
our world? It is no exaggeration to say that Alexandrian science
laid all future western science under a debt, and forms the basis
of the scientific world-view of the West to this day.

But the city embraced very much more than its planning, its
building and the history of its intellectual success. Alexandria
grew into the largest city of the Mediterranean world, with a
population somewhere between half a million and a million. It
became a bewildering and bruising collection of peoples, in

which (according to Polybius) there were three main elements: the native Egyptians, 'sharp-witted and well suited to civil life'; the mercenary soldiers, the adventurers and the place-hunters who were often riotous and a constant threat to good order; and lastly the 'Alexandrines' who were at least Greek by origin and 'had not forgotten the general Greek way of life'. There were also several ethnic enclaves, roughly homogeneous, and a influential community of Jews in the quarter known as Delta, close to the royal palaces. Besides these more or less permanent communities, there was a shifting population from almost every country of the known world with an interest in trade, advancement, pleasure or the fruits of the mind.

Too often, this became an incendiary mixture of peoples and cultures. The settled Greekness of the place, which might have been a force for stability in the early days of the Ptolemies, was later fractured by sudden movements, by influx and exits pushed or pulled by the magnetic force of the city itself. Nor was the 'Greek way of life' that had the approval of Polybius always an influence for good. There was a frivolous and dangerous side to Greek social life that showed itself in luxury, spectacle, games, feasts, and a love of fashionable thrills. Greeks were also adept at plotting and scheming, fickle in their affections, and no strangers to violence. Theocritus in one of his idylls celebrated the peaceful order of Alexandria in the time of Ptolemy II: 'Nowadays we are safe in the streets from Egyptian rogues. The tricks those rascals used to play!' He spoke much too soon. The pleasure-loving kings used spectacle and public entertainment as a part of state policy. But every concession to this public hunger for thrills only sharpened the riotous and brutal appetite of the mob.

Ptolemy II, after a triumphant march deep into the lands of the Seleucid empire, had identified himself with Dionysus, the

Thracian god of drunken revelry who had also conducted a giddy and mysterious progress throughout the East. The identification stuck, and Dionysian revels became an essential part in the success of the Ptolemaeia, the festival of the god-kings held every four years. In the festival, the figure of Dionysus was mounted on an elephant, garlanded and with the ivy-clad wand of the *thyrsus* in his hand, while a rabble of satyrs and maenads followed in his wake. In a famous account of the third Ptolemaeia, when a procession of 75,000 people took two days to cross the city, we see a 3-metre-high statue of the god, clad in purple, ladling wine from a golden bowl that held nearly 400 litres. Three hundred men pulled another float bearing a wine press trampled by 60 satyrs, treading in time to music.

All this was potent propaganda for the ruling house, but in time it became more a drug for the people. Public orgy became part of public expectation, and violence and sudden death inevitably followed. Pandered to by drink and lavish spectacle, the Alexandrian mob developed a taste for blood. In 59 BC the historian Diodorus Siculus saw a Roman torn apart in the street because he had accidentally killed a cat, one of the sacred animals of Egypt. More and more, mob violence entered into the intrigues of the Ptolemies. Incitement towards assassination was part of routine policy. Ptolemy VI barely escaped from the plots of a certain Dionysus Petosarapis. In 80 BC, when Ptolemy XI murdered his co-ruler, who was his wife and his cousin, after reigning for only 19 days, the mob hauled him from the palace to the gymnasium and killed him also.

The victory of mob rule showed the extent of the social and political sickness in Egypt and in the capital. It put a stamp of defeat on the long, declining era of the Ptolemies. For the ordinary Egyptian life was becoming poorer and harder, and the road through the maze of the bureaucracy was a woeful pilgrimage. The account of one Apollonius, attempting in 157 BC to secure a military post for which he was eligible, was a painful reminder of official futility. Round and round he went among offices and office-holders, writing, petitioning, cajoling, fetching, begging. His letters needed wings, so far was the distance they were forced to travel:

> They were delivered for the *dioiketes* to read, and I received back the *prostagma* from Ptolemy, and the letter from Epimenides. And I took them to Isidorus the *autoteles*, and from him I carried them to Philoxenus, and from him to Artemon, and from him to Lycus, who made a rough draft, which I took to Sarapion in the office of the *epistolographus*, and from him to Eubius, and from him to Dorion, and he made another draft, and then back again to Sarapion, and all handed back to be read by the *dioiketes*.

Nor was that the end of the matter. The little piece of business drifted through another list of idle hands until it disappeared from the record, still unresolved.

By 118 BC the ferocious rivalries of the royal house and the slipshod incompetence of the administration had produced such a wretched state in society, so much violence and confusion, that Ptolemy VIII Physkon and his warring queen Cleopatra II were forced to try to wipe out the wrongs of the past by a decree that promised a widespread amnesty for criminals and wrongdoers, a remission of taxes and relief from various duties and dues, a confirmation of doubtful landtitles, a right to rebuild destroyed properties, a new freedom from the exactions of officials, severe new penalties for law-breakers, and in general the promise of quiet enjoyment for all decent citizens in the lawful conduct of their affairs.

But these large promises could not be met. The complaints continued.

Many people [a high official wrote to an underling] are still writing against you, your subordinates, and especially the tax-farmers, for abuse of power and fraudulent exactions and even blackmail.

The state system so successfully established by the first three Ptolemies was slowly disintegrating, and events seemed to bear out old pharaonic prophecies: 'Everywhere there will be harm. The seasons will remain in darkness. Even by day, what is light and what is shadow?'

The world of the eastern Mediterranean was in turmoil. Old kingdoms struggled against the baleful ambition of Rome. Constant wars, large and small, cut off the export markets on which the prosperity of Egypt depended so much. Social unrest harmed agricultural production. Peasant cultivators refused to work. They took sanctuary in the old temples, particularly in the Thebaid. Canals were not dredged, dykes not maintained, and water-wheels unrepaired. The delicate balance of land and water in the Nile valley was disturbed, with serious consequences. The coinage was debased again and again, copper coins replacing silver or gold, and inflation increased. In Upper Egypt whole regions asserted an autonomy against the Ptolemaic court in Alexandria. For a time, a certain Pharaoh Harmachis declared an independent state in the territory between the Nile cataracts.

To support them in this sea of troubles the later Ptolemies had little beyond an effete confidence in the god-given right to rule, and an increasing resort to violence. They came down harshly on their own subjects. 'Again and again', it was said of Ptolemy Physkon, 'he turned his troops on the people of

Alexandria and massacred them.' Their own people they might destroy, but in the face of the Roman threat the Ptolemies were so weak they could only watch aghast. They tried to combine cringing submission with futile stratagems. Neither worked. In 164 BC Ptolemy VI was seen trudging up the Capitol hill in Rome, pitifully dressed, no more impressive than the meanest petitioner. The will of his brother Ptolemy VIII offered Egypt to Rome, if the king should die without issue. To explain this astonishing gift to the disbelieving Roman senators, he displayed on his fat body scars supposedly made by his own ungrateful subjects. For this demonstration Physkon got nothing but contempt. When Scipio Aemilianus visited Alexandria and saw the puffed-up king waddling anxiously forward, he commented to his companion: 'The citizens of Alexandria owe me one thing. At last they have seen their king walk!'

In the squalor of their lives, one fat king followed another. Ptolemy XI, who dared to call himself Alexander, was so gross he needed an attendant on each side to support him. Yet it was said that when he was drunk he was agile enough in lewd dances. Indecency, in body and mind, became the measure of rule. It was rumoured that Physkon had chopped up his son and sent the body in a box to the child's mother as a present. The rumour was believed, for had not this king who called himself the Benefactor been retitled Kakergetes (Malefactor) by his people? In the Ptolemaic family warfare went on, kings against queens, children against parents, brothers against sisters. Incestuous marriages were made and broken for a momentary advantage. When the great Ptolemy II Philadelphus had begun the fashion of incest by marrying his sister Arsinoe II, he had so shocked the ancient world that the Thracian poet Sotades had rudely commented: 'Now you've thrust your prick into an unholy opening.' For this the poet was caught, bound in a

wooden box and drowned at sea. But when Ptolemy IX Lathyrus, the king known as Chick-Pea, set his sights on his own
granddaughter, there was hardly a murmur of surprise.

Suddenly, despite the variety of the royal couplings, the
direct male line in the Ptolemies was at an end. In 80 BC, when
the Alexandrian mob murdered Ptolemy XI Alexander, the
only remaining males of royal blood were two illegitimate
sons of Ptolemy IX Soter by a concubine. To forestall any
Roman intervention, the people of Alexandria quickly
acclaimed one of these young men as king of Egypt, and the
other as king of Cyprus. Unusually, Ptolemy XII was crowned
in Alexandria not Memphis, perhaps because haste and safety
required it, and he was given a queen, Cleopatra V, who
according to custom was probably his sister. He took the
resounding title of New Dionysus, but the Alexandrians in
their blunt way called him Nothos the Bastard, while in the
world at large he was known as Auletes the Flute Player.

A king who assumed the name Dionysus and earned the
nickname Flute Player gave notice of an artistic temperament.
The cult of Dionysus, enthusiastically taken up by many eastern kings, meant several different things. At the most serious
level, it indicated an identification with a mystery-god, one
who beneath the conventions of day-to-day religion reconciled beliefs in a deep, unspoken faith. In this faith the attributes of true divinity, obscurely manifest in Dionysus or Isis or
Osiris, were immanent in the new god-king. Ptolemy Auletes
was the 'new Osiris' in Egyptian hieroglyphic inscriptions,
and as such he was likely to have taken a serious interest in the
meaning and symbolism of his coronation.

I went to the house of the Greek kings [the high priest of Ptah
recorded] which is on the shore of the Great Sea by Rhakotis.

[45]

There I crowned in his royal palace the king of Upper and
Lower Egypt, the Master of two worlds, the Father-and-
Sister-loving God, the New Osiris. He went to the temple of
the Lady Isis. He offered her many and costly sacrifices.

There is no need to doubt that these were authentic acts of
worship by the young king.

But there was another disreputable side to the cult of
Dionysus that Auletes was glad to acknowledge. In honour of
this god of excess, who goaded his followers to the wildest
dances, the heaviest drinking and the boldest sexuality, Auletes
was ready to play his flute the night through, to dance and
drink with the most fervent of them. He changed into female
clothes, as Dionysus had done, and flaunted himself recklessly,
and he was offended in his cups when others refused the
indulgence of his orgies. The philosopher Demetrius, a man
of stiff sobriety who tried to avoid the court frolics, only managed to appease the pleasure-loving king (a man known for
casual cruelty) by dancing before him each day in a wanton,
transparent gown. Though Auletes fathered several children,
he took his sexual experiments far enough to gain a reputation
for homosexuality. On a stele at Philae certain Egyptian men
claimed that they had slept with the king.

Egypt needed something more in these hard days than a
Dionysian monarch. Rome was laying claim to the kingdom
on the basis of some dubious documents and refused to recog-
nize Auletes. Two young princes from the East, the sons of
Cleopatra Selene who was the only legitimate Ptolemy left
alive, were in Rome pressing their own claims by bribery on
the greedy senators. But Rome had no wish to unite the
Ptolemaic and Seleucid kingdoms. The senators pocketed the
bribes and packed the youths off on a homeward journey

through Sicily, where they were thoroughly robbed. Uneasily, Auletes matched his rivals in Rome, bribe for bribe. The great men in Rome grew rich on Egyptian money while the treasury at Alexandria, made lean by the deteriorating Egyptian economy, was drained to no purpose. The Roman nobles were pleased to despise the softness and oriental luxury of the king whose bribes they so gladly accepted.

At any moment the Roman thunder might break over Egypt. The storm was held off, not by Auletes' guile, but by jealousy and indecision within Rome. A great internal strife was underway there, concerning the very nature of the republic itself, and there was a feeling that other matters could wait. Egypt would have its turn. In the meantime Ptolemy Auletes dabbled in waters whose troubled currents he could not control. He sent 8000 cavalry to help the general Pompey in Palestine, since Pompey was the Roman in the ascendant in the lands nearest to Egypt. Already Pompey had crushed Tigranes and Mithridates, troublesome enemies to Rome in Armenia, Pontus and Syria. In 64 BC Pompey extinguished the Seleucid line and brought Syria to Rome as a province. The old Queen Cleopatra Selene was dead, captured and killed by Tigranes on the Euphrates in 69 BC. Illegitimate Auletes, only shakily a Ptolemy, hated or despised at home and abroad, under the displeasure of Rome and watching that military giant flex dangerous muscles nearby, knew then the impotence and loneliness of his position.

In 69 BC Ptolemy Auletes fathered a baby girl, his third child, who was called Cleopatra according to the custom of the family. At about the same time the king's wife, also Cleopatra, disappeared from the Egyptian records. Perhaps she died, perhaps she was put away, a fate not unknown to the co-rulers of the Ptolemies. Was this queen, Cleopatra V, the

mother of the baby Cleopatra? It is not known. The father
had a reputation for sexual looseness. At the very beginning of
her life there is an unanswered question about Cleopatra. We
can only see her as her father's daughter, with all that entails,
for we are in doubt about her mother.

In the search for Cleopatra, her father Ptolemy Auletes will
certainly take us some of the way, though the historical sources
are silent on her childhood and upbringing. She was a
Ptolemy, raised in the Ptolemaic court, in the city of Alexandria. She had within reach every luxury, every refinement
known to the ancient world. Egypt was still wealthy, though it
had been richer, and it is the habit of decadent courts in declining economies to let a painted face try to hide bodily decay.

What, then, were some of the antecedents to her character,
the grounds for the formation of her mature being? Her
father was a man of artistic sensibility and talent. His nickname, Flute Player, though a contemptuous comment on the
king, was in its way a compliment to the man. In music, in
dance, in the theatre of his decorative, indulgent life, Auletes
showed real ability. He understood the part of statecraft that
uses the propaganda of public entertainment, and he knew
how much of entertainment was glitter and subterfuge. He
had the weakness of his vices but also the intelligence to judge
events; and though he did not have the force of character to
stand up to them, he had the slipperiness to avoid the worst
consequences. The world boiled dangerously around him; he
was disliked at home in Alexandria and despised abroad; yet
despite many setbacks, amid court plots and Roman intimidation, he clung to the throne for 29 years.

It is easy to see what counted against Auletes – his
debauchery, his frivolity, his extravagance, his self-absorption,
his cruelty. To find threads of virtue in the dismal cloth of his

life is much harder. Yet in an aesthetic sensibility, vice and virtue are often only two sides of the same coin. For men of this kind religion and theatre are not far apart. Both deal with shadowlands beyond the worst materialism of the senses. Auletes seemed by instinct to tap into the springs of Egyptian religion, both the ancestral practices of the pharaonic state and the mystery-faith of a Dionysian god-king.

> The crypts of the great temple of Denderah, which Lathyrus and Ptolemy Alexander had not finished, were completed by Auletes; he set up an altar at Coptos to Khem, Isis and Heh; put his name more than once on the temples at Karnak [Thebes]; set up bronze-bound gates at the great pylon of Edfu; enlarged Ptolemy Philometor's temple at Kom Ombo.

This was the work of a man deeply imbued with the spirit of Egypt, and it is no surprise to find at Philae, on the island in the Nile, a mighty statue of Auletes as pharaoh, the lord and governor of the ancient land. No doubt this understanding of the symbols and forms of Egyptian religion, so important to the native people to whom Alexandria meant almost nothing, helped Auletes to keep his precarious hold on the throne for so long. It was appropriate, too, that there should be at Philae an inscription from a certain Tryphon, 'catamite of the Young Dionysus'.

The character of her father Auletes, his vices and virtues, entered into the character of Cleopatra. And growing up in the court, she took the things that the court had to offer. Her health and physical well-being would have been in the hands of the best Alexandrian doctors. There were no better doctors in the West or the Near East. Her tutors would have come from the community of scholars living almost in the shade of the palace, in the halls of the Museum and the Library.

There, the pursuit of knowledge went quietly on, despite the depravity of the court. A Ptolemy attack on artists and scholars, such as Physkon had made, seemed an offence against nature. Had not the house of Ptolemy perjured itself, and effected a swindle for which it forfeited a large amount of gold, to bring to the Museum from Athens the best and oldest manuscripts of the Greek genius? That Greek hunger for learning did not die just because the kings lost political and moral sense.

The events of her later life gave good evidence that Cleopatra had the quick wits and the guile of the Ptolemies. From the historian Plutarch we know, too, that she was well-educated, even learned:

> There were few of the barbarian nations that she had to answer through an interpreter. To most of them she spoke directly, as for example to the Ethiopians, Troglodytes, Hebrews, Arabians, Syrians, Medes, Parthians, and many others whose language she had learnt. And all this was the more surprising in that most of her predecessors, the Ptolemies, scarcely gave themselves the trouble of acquiring the tongue of Egypt.

To the natural talents of a Ptolemy she had added something else, a resolution, a staying-power, an extra hardness and purpose that echoed the great queens of the past. She had in her the fire of Arsinoe II, of the second and third Cleopatras.

To the formal schooling gained by a young girl within the palace walls, the city of Alexandria added an education of another kind. But the huge city spoke in different voices and the whole message was not easy to grasp. On the one hand, Alexandria seemed to represent the highest point of contemporary civilization, a place of grandeur and intellect unrivalled in all lands of the West and the Near East. In the majesty of its public buildings and palaces, in the convenient order of its streets, in the ingenuity of its harbours, canals and waterways, in its free associations, universal trade and enquiring spirit it stood as a monument to what could be done when Macedonian energy and Greek talent were married to Egyptian life and money. The daily prospect of the city that opened before the eyes of each Ptolemy must have seemed to a young member of the ruling house a complete justification for so many years of Ptolemaic government. Seeing all this, which one of them would not have desired and worked for the continuation of their dynasty?

On the other hand, Alexandria had for a long time shown the symptoms of urban disease. It was superficial and restless, full of empty spectacle and expense, seeking diversion at all costs. Within its many districts were little wars, shifting violence swirling in and out of ethnic enclaves, places that were almost ghettos. The dangerous mob was easily stirred by demagogues and faction leaders into cruelty and bloodletting. Among the people cynicism and moral laxity mirrored the vices of the kings. Alexandria was a place of distorting mirrors throwing back at the citizens caricatures of humanity. In late days, too, a smell of fear seeped through the city, coming out of the royal quarter of Brucheion, and induced by the vicious distractions of a divided royal family. In this suffocating atmosphere an intelligent girl could see the meaning of failure, how easily greatness of spirit degenerated into mere criminal aptitude.

As Cleopatra grew into her teenage years there was truly much to fear in the state of king and country. In 59 BC, when Julius Caesar was one of the Roman consuls, Ptolemy Auletes bought his support with a payment of 6000 talents, a sum of money so gigantic it was said to equal about half the yearly revenue of Egypt. At last, Auletes was recognized as Egyptian monarch and declared to be 'ally and friend of the Roman people'. Caesar, Pompey and Crassus were now joined together in the First Triumvirate, a dictatorial conjunction that cut across all the traditions of republican Rome. Auletes was recognized in Egypt, but his brother who ruled in Cyprus, and who had neglected to pay bribes, was not so lucky. The tribune Clodius, one of Caesar's men, moved a law to annex Cyprus, and Marcus Cato was sent to take over the island. In exchange for his throne, the Cypriot Ptolemy was offered the high priesthood of the temple of Aphrodite at Paphos. The king preferred to commit suicide.

With his empire diminished by the loss of Cyprus, and by the surrender of Cyrene on the North African coast, Auletes faced the anger of the Alexandrian mob. The people had already seen the treasury ravaged for Roman bribes, and now could hardly believe the indifference of the king to the death of his brother and the loss of his territory. Auletes thought it wise to leave the country. In 58 BC he set out for Rome, hoping to raise money against the surety of the Egyptian economy, and seeking further assurances of support. On the way to Italy, Auletes met Cato at Rhodes and was received by the famous Stoic sitting on a commode and emptying his Roman bowels. Auletes knew then, from close quarters, the class of people he was forced to deal with.

For two years, until 57 BC, Auletes was in Rome, or at a villa belonging to Pompey in the Alban hills, caught in the labyrinth of Roman politics. Without the resources of his treasury in Alexandria, in any case seriously depleted, Auletes had to borrow heavily to cover his schemes. In a short time he was deeply in debt to the financier Rabirius Postumus.

The populace in Alexandria had no wish to see the return of the king. In his absence they recognized the queens, first the shadowy figure of Cleopatra VI, who was either Auletes' wife or eldest daughter, and then when she died they brought forward his second daughter Berenice IV. A deputation under the philosopher Dio was sent to Rome to plead for the dynastic change in Alexandria. But Auletes hired thugs to attack the party at the landing in the bay of Naples. Several were killed, and though Dio escaped he was too frightened to deliver the message in Rome. He was caught and murdered soon after. Having expended his bribes and done what murder could do, Auletes discreetly retired from Rome to the sacred precinct of Artemis at Ephesus. Here, he was close to the Roman legions in the East, ready to take the advantage of any wind.

In Rome, the triumvirs were divided on the question of Egypt. Early in 56 BC lightning struck the statue of Jupiter on Mount Alban, and when the Sibylline Books were opened to see what this portent meant, a message cautiously sympathetic to Auletes was revealed. It was decided that Ptolemy Auletes should be helped to recover his throne, but by whom and under what conditions were matters still subject to jealous rivalry. At last, one of Pompey's followers, Aulus Gabinius, proconsul of the newly formed Roman province of Syria, was chosen to see Auletes home. The chief condition of this help was that the Egyptian king should pay the truly fantastic sum of 10,000 talents, part of which was ear-marked for both Caesar and Pompey. The moneylender Rabirius, anxious for the security of his loans, put aside Roman business and decided to accompany Gabinius into Egypt.

In Alexandria, the news that the king was returning pleased no one. To block the return the citizens quickly searched for some prince to marry the young queen Berenice. A youth of respectable Seleucid parentage was discovered but he proved to be so hopelessly vulgar that the city wits called him *Kybiosaktes*, the Salt Fishmonger, and Berenice found that the only remedy for him was to take him out and have him strangled. Then another young man with better manners was tried. At the end of 56 BC Archelaus, who claimed to be the illegitimate son of the great Pontic king Mithridates, married Berenice and slipped uneasily onto the Ptolemaic throne.

Archelaus had acted without Roman permission and could expect no mercy for this boldness. In the spring of 55 BC Gabinius marched into Egypt along the desert corridor between Palestine and Pelusium on the Nile delta. He had in his train Ptolemy Auletes, and the commander of his cavalry was a burly, confident fellow named Mark Antony, already experienced and proven in the field though he was only 26 years old. Archelaus made a stand against the Roman army and was killed in battle. Auletes was brought in triumph to Alexandria and began at once to settle old scores. The usurper Archelaus was dead and given honourable burial, against Auletes' wishes, on the insistence of Mark Antony. But Berenice was too implicated in opposition to expect any fatherly tenderness. With the usual Ptolemaic ruthlessness, Auletes ordered her execution.

Auletes now had four children left. Eldest was Cleopatra, a girl of 14. Her sister Arsinoe was a little younger, and her two brothers, both bearing the dynastic name Ptolemy, were only six and four. Nothing is known of Cleopatra in the years of her father's exile, but she had survived and now could expect the succession to the throne, very likely as co-ruler with her little brother. But her inheritance looked insecure and full of dangers. She could not have helped but notice the misery of her country, in civil war and under a faltering economy, to which was added the crushing burden of the debt owed to Rabirius. In the turmoil of mutual hatreds she saw the insolence of the Romans, for only Gabinius and his army, now garrisoned in Alexandria, stood between the king and the resentment of the people. To an intelligent girl it was clear enough that, though Auletes sat on the throne in Alexandria, the spoils of Egypt had fallen to Rome.

Rome had brought the king back and now Romans wanted payment. Rabirius, the chief creditor, was given the post of *dioiketes*, or minister of finance for all of Egypt. In no time he had begun an expert and wholesale plunder of state resources, so much so that he barely avoided lynching by the outraged mob and was forced to flee back to Rome. He was joined there by Gabinius who also had dipped his hand deep in the Egyptian pocket. In Rome, both men were put on trial for financial irregularity and for defrauding the Roman people. With the connivance of Julius Caesar, and defended by the orator Cicero (who had formerly called Gabinius a thieving dancing-boy in paint and hair-curlers), the two men were let off lightly. Caesar undertook to recover the Egyptian debt owed to Rabirius – money borrowed by Auletes largely to bribe Caesar himself – and in this way gained a powerful future interest in Egyptian affairs.

Ptolemy XII Auletes, the New Dionysus, died in the early summer of 51 BC, within four years of his restoration and aged about fifty-five. The contempt that he received from the Romans was well-earned, and the anger shown to him by the people of Alexandria was so constant that he had to see out his reign under the protection of Gabinius' troops, who had stayed on in Egypt after the departure of their general. He was resigned to his position, merely a puppet-king of a Roman client-state. He made his will and sent it to be lodged with the Vestal Virgins in Rome, who were the guardians of the state archives. He left his kingdom, under Roman supervision, to his children, his son Ptolemy XIII aged ten, and his daughter Cleopatra VII aged eighteen.

3

THE SHADOW
OF ROME

IN THE FOURTH CENTURY BC Aristotle, that universal
intelligence of the ancient world, thought that Rome was
a Greek city. The town on the hills halfway up the leg of Italy
was too dim a place to be noticed in the starry firmament of
Greek civilization. In those days, the flow of ideas and
influence went only one way, so it seemed no more than a
course of nature that the Romans imported wholesale the
pantheon of Greece to become their own gods under other
names. How ironic, then, was the development presided over
by those joint gods, but with such unequal favour. A Greek
historian at the beginning of the Christian era would have
looked back to see with surprise that all the lands of the eastern Mediterranean world conquered and fostered by Greeks,
almost to the gates of India, were now in the possession of the
unbending, unimaginative rustics from Rome.

The attractions for Rome in the East were not difficult to
see. The republic had an instinctive purpose, particularly after
the defeat of Carthage, to push dominion as far as arms and
armies could reach. For this hardy people, safety lay in aggres-

sion. But war required money, and nowhere was there such a profusion of riches than in the lands under the superior culture of the Greeks, especially in Ptolemaic Egypt. The picture that the orator Dio of Prusa gave of Alexandria, which was a true portrait for most of the age of the Ptolemies, was a cause of greed and envy in a money-minded people:

> Not only do you have a monopoly [wrote Dio to his favourite city] of the entire Mediterranean shipping because of the beauty of your harbours, the vast size of your fleet, and the abundance of the products of every land that you handle, but also you have in your grasp the outer waters that lie beyond, in the Red Sea and the Indian Ocean . . . The trade of almost the whole world is yours. For Alexandria is placed, as it were, at the crossroads of the world, a market bringing together all men into one place.

This world was a matter of amazement to less prosperous peoples. The mosaic that some anonymous hand, around 100 BC, laid in a villa at Palestrina in Italy (see Plates 4 and 5) showed a wistful Egyptian topography for Romans to dream on. In this representation the great Nile flowed broad and calm and alive with curious boats, drifting through stately jungles, past temples and palaces where the rituals were leisurely and exotic but powerfully redolent of the sweet smell of money. From an early time, perhaps by the start of the third century BC, many Roman feet itched to take the road to that happy land.

At first, the policy of the Ptolemies was to be cordial but uncommitted towards Rome. Soon after 275 BC, when a Roman army had forced Egypt to take notice with an attack on the king of Epirus, Ptolemy II sent an embassy to Rome with a cautious offer of friendship. The patrician Quintus

Ogulnius made the return journey with the acknowledgement of *amicitia* that Ptolemy had sought. Ten years later, when the first great contest between Rome and Carthage began, Carthage asked her rich North African neighbour for a loan. Ptolemy refused. He said both sides were his friends, but he would be glad to act as mediator between them.

Neutrality and 'friendship' to Rome were carefully maintained by successive Ptolemies. But the stance became more precarious after the decisive struggle between Hannibal and Scipio Africanus led to the victory of Rome in the second Punic War. At that time, in 217 BC, Agelaus of Aetolia clearly warned his fellow Greek powers that unless they combined they would be swept away by either Carthage or Rome. It was in the character of the Ptolemies, and part of their policy, to do nothing. The moment passed. Envoys came to Alexandria from Rome looking for grain, since the fields of Italy were laid waste by war. There was nothing in the doctrine of neutrality that precluded the making of profits, and so grain was provided. Romans in their bulky robes, so ungainly compared to the smart, short tunics of the Greeks, became familiar enough in the streets of Alexandria. Roman-trained soldiers, many from the confederate Italian tribes, took service in Egyptian armies. There were many of these soldiers about, for the Roman legions were on the march again in the East, contesting the power of the Macedonian Philip and the Seleucid Antiochus.

Once more, Egypt stood aside. Sympathy for fellow Greeks suggested aid for Philip and Antiochus (though both these ambitious rulers had it in mind to dismember the outlying parts of the Egyptian realms), but for the Ptolemies fear of Rome, or at least the wish not to offend, was stronger than Greek fellow-feeling. In return for this neutrality, Rome did

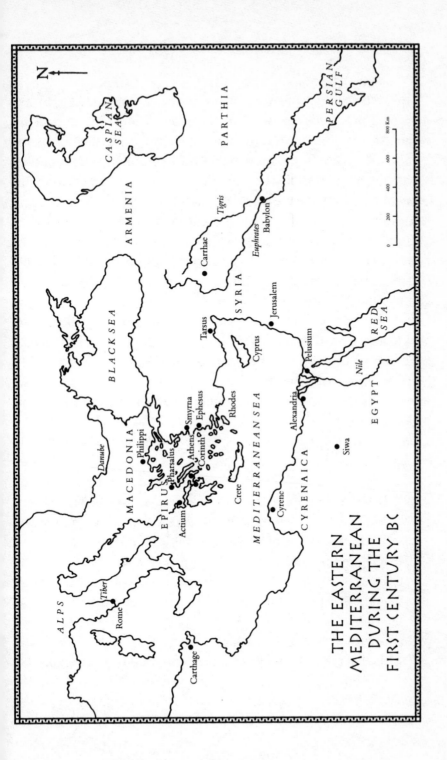

THE EASTERN
MEDITERRANEAN
DVRING THE
FIRST CENTVRY B(

warn Antiochus that Egypt lay under the protection of her *amicitia* but made no move to force the Seleucid king to hand back the Ptolemaic territory he had seized. And when Antiochus the Great was defeated and broken, Egypt received nothing from the distribution of his lands to the friends of Rome, though the Ptolemies dearly wanted the strategic coast-land of Coele-Syria (Palestine). It had come to this: Rome could afford to take Egypt for granted.

Thirty years later, when another Antiochus – Epiphanes – made repeated attacks on Egypt, and in 168 BC had gone so far as to take Memphis and lay siege to Alexandria, the brothers Ptolemy VI and VIII owed the preservation of their kingdom to Roman contempt for the wretched squabbles of orientals. The story was told by the historian Polybius. In 168 BC, after the crushing victory of the legions over Macedonia at Pydna, the Roman envoy Popilius Laenas confronted King Antiochus in the Alexandrian suburb of Eleusis and informed him of the decision of the Roman senate, that the Seleucid king should break off his campaign and leave Egypt.

> When the king read this communication he said he wished to consult his counsellors, but Popilius stopped him and did something that seemed overbearing and utterly arrogant. Having in his hand a staff made from a vine-shoot, he drew a circle around Antiochus with this cane and told him that he would not leave the circle until he had given his reply. The king was astonished by this action, and without words for a short time. Then he said he would do what the Romans wished. At that, Popilius embraced him warmly as a friend.

With this simple act the hand of Rome began to draw the final curtain on the experiment with Hellenism that Alexander the Great had so triumphantly initiated nearly two centuries before. The Greek-speaking peoples knew then the new rulers of their eastern world.

The act was done, but the implications and the full understanding of it only came to view slowly. Immediately, what became abundantly clear was the insolent power of Rome and the abject capitulation of the house of Ptolemy to that authority. After Antiochus was expelled by the word of the senate, the two Ptolemies who contested the kingship and the Alexandrian mob continued their triple dance of intrigue, agitation and revolt. In 164 BC the better of the kings, Ptolemy VI Philometor, fled to Rome seeking help. He cut a sad figure for the monarch of the richest of all Mediterranean lands. Diodorus pictured his miserable arrival in Rome:

> Ptolemy, king of Egypt, having been thrown from his kingdom by his own brother, arrived in Rome in the pitiful guise of a simple citizen, with one eunuch and three slaves. He lodged with a certain Demetrius who lived, because of the high city rents, in a little garret at the top of a mean house. Who would then put his trust in the blessings of the world, or call happy those whose prosperity exceeds measure?

The determination of the senate regarding the rival kings, reached after the usual evasions and bribery, seems to have been accepted, and perhaps prevented further strife and bloodshed in Alexandria. But at what cost to the sovereignty, dignity and reputation of once-mighty Egypt? But reality teaches lessons. Fawning inscriptions began to appear in Greek lands applauding Romans as 'the common benefactors of all Greeks'. And there was a certain dismal truth to this for the ordinary Greek populace, given the ineptitude of their own rulers. Even the Greek historian Polybius, a judicious and fair-minded man who lived through these times, found himself leaning towards Rome with enthusiasm. The increasing dominance of Rome in the East, he wrote, was 'the fairest and most widely advantageous stroke of fortune' for all. There was safety, at least, under the Roman cloak.

This new reality in the East, though still disputed by some independently-minded Greeks such as the islanders of Rhodes, was grudgingly acknowledged by most. But there was no joy in the acknowledgement, and Alexandrians, more than most, felt their helplessness in the new polity. A high Egyptian official, who had taken part in negotiations with Romans, wrote with sullen resignation of those outsiders 'who are turning their forces against every place' and becoming 'stewards of the wealth of others'. But much of the fault, the writer went on, lay with the native inhabitants, 'for indolence is unable to preserve freedom for any length of time'. The march of Rome was relentless, as the bold empires of Carthage and Macedonia had discovered to their cost. In the Egyptian view, rather than face the waste of war against such grim opponents, it was better to be respectful, flexible and accommodating, for who knew where the legions might go next?

There was constant fear, leading from time to time to panic, that Rome desired Egypt. Good economic and political reasons suggested that this might be so, and the Ptolemies and their advisers were men of subtle imagination who could read the maximum into each sign. Roman intentions seemed to be revealed by such events as the visit made by Scipio Aemilianus to Egypt towards the end of 140 BC. Here was a great man, a representative of the patrician family that had done famous service to the republic. He was a Hellenist who spoke Greek well, a man of culture who knew the literature and philosophy of Greece. But why was he in Egypt? When the citizens of Alexandria looked on his distinguished person they saw in the background, in their minds' eye, the burning walls of Carthage and the death of old empire.

The historian Diodorus recorded the visit:

Scipio and his colleagues arrived in Egypt intending to look at all the kingdom. Ptolemy received them with great ceremony and careful forethought, preparing sumptuous banquets. He took them around the palace and showed them the royal quarters and the treasury. But the Roman envoys were men of sobriety and virtue, who ate only such little amounts of food as was good for their health, and despised luxurious living as corrupting to both body and soul.

So passing over the wonders shown them by the king as things not worth examination, they showed a keen interest in things of real importance, such as the disposition of the city, the arrangements of its wealth, and the particular construction of the Pharos lighthouse. Then they sailed up the river and noted carefully the richness of the land and the role of the Nile in this prosperity. They saw the numerous cities throughout Egypt, the vast number of the people, the defensive advantages of the country, and the outstanding quality of the land as a whole. They saw how well-planned it was for safe and powerful government. Marvelling at all these advantages, they understood how a mighty state could be maintained there, if only the rulers were up to the mark.

Clearly, this visit was more spying than diplomacy. But in the report that Rome received, as Diodorus outlined it, there was a quandary for Romans to ponder. The incompetence and the luxurious corruption of the rulers invited an invasion, but the natural strength of Egypt, its wealth, its stable society and its military advantages recommended caution. And caution was a Roman watchword. One of their more recent heroes, Quintus Fabius, owed success and everlasting fame to a stratagem that won him the admired title of Cunctator, the Delayer. Rome did not like to move without long consideration and a careful weighing of opposites. At what point did the chaos of foolish leadership tip the balance against natural strengths given by history and geography? Until that decision was ready to be made Rome kept a watching brief, while the court and the mob in Alexandria, nervous and conspiracy-minded at the best of times, found no shortage of bitter tastes to feed their paranoia.

So Romans in Egypt received careful consideration. Officials, even unimportant functionaries, were looked after with exaggerated respect. The way was swept smooth for them, as was indicated by a letter from the Fayum in 112 BC:

> To Asclepiades. Be informed that Lucius Memmius, a Roman senator, a person of position and dignity, is sailing from Alexandria to the district of Arsinoe to see the sights. Let him be received with special ceremony. Take care that in all the proper places the guest-rooms are prepared and the landing-places are ready, and present him there with the gifts listed below. Make sure there is furniture in the guest-rooms. Provide tit-bits for him to give Petesouchos the crocodile-god and the crocodiles, and arrange for the viewing of the Labyrinth, with all the offering and sacrifices that will be needed. In short, do your very best and take the greatest pains to see that this visitor is well-satisfied.

In time, the spirit of appeasement became more a disease than a policy – a melancholy way of life. There is evidence of

A selection of coins from the Ptolemaic period

TOP LEFT: This coin dates from the reign of Ptolemy I, the first Ptolemaic pharaoh who was one of Alexander the Great's generals, and depicts Alexander the Great in a carriage drawn by elephants.

TOP RIGHT: Coin depicting Ptolemy I.

CENTRE LEFT: Ptolemy II and his wife, Arsinoe II.

CENTRE RIGHT: Ptolemy III.

BELOW: Bronze coin of Cleopatra VII. Coin portraits of Cleopatra are some of the few contemporary representations of the queen.

ABOVE: Wall painting showing threshing corn in Ancient Egypt. From the Tomb of Menena at Thebes, 18th Dynasty (1567–1320 BC). Roman travellers noted the rich land bordering the Nile as they sailed up the great river.

BELOW: The Nile Valley still benefits from the all-important flood waters to irrigate the land and make it rich and fertile, as it did thousands of years ago in Ancient Egypt.

This watercolour by Harold Oakley illustrates the famous late 19th-century
reconstruction of the Pharos of Alexandria which was built in the reign of
Ptolemy II to help seafarers locate the entrance to Alexandria's harbour along
the flat Egyptian coastline. The tower was built on the island of Pharos and
it was soon acknowledged as one of the seven wonders of the ancient world.
The lighthouse has now been destroyed and this reconstruction was based
on the best scholarly evidence available at the time.

Dating from the 1st century BC, the Palestrina floor mosaic was found in the Roman town of Praeneste (Palestrina) in southern Italy and shows how from an early age Egypt was a popular theme in Roman works of art. It provides a rare view of an idealized landscape of the Upper Nile. The southern part of the Nile Valley is represented by the exotic animals in the upper section of the mosaic while the foreground depicts the Nile delta. Various Egyptian papyrus boats are shown sailing up and down the river, while Egyptian and Greek temples line the banks.

The image of Cleopatra as a
tragic vamp which persists
today was aided by imaginative
artists through the centuries.

FACING PAGE: *Study of a nude
woman as Cleopatra*, a drawing by
Rembrandt van Rijn (1606–1669).

ABOVE: *Cleopatra*
by Pietro Dandini (1646–1712).

LEFT: Engraving of Cleopatra
by Chapman 1804.

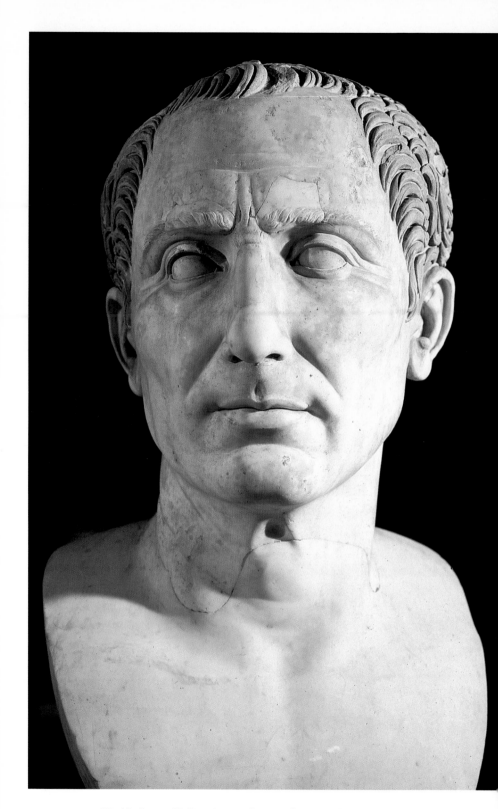

Marble bust of Julius Caesar showing him as a figure of authority.
Dictator from 48–44 BC, his affair with Cleopatra helped to hasten his downfall.

this afflicted spirit in the attempts to please (and not only in Egypt) in which a ruler would bequeath his kingdom to Rome under certain circumstances. Ptolemy VIII Physkon, desperate for Roman support, wrote in his will:

> If I should suffer the inevitable lot of man before leaving a heir to the throne, I bequeath the royal power that belongs to me to the Romans, always my faithful partners in friendship and treaty.

It was a tactic to buy support and time, and it was used by others in the East with reason to fear Rome, for example Nicomedes of Bithynia and Attalus of Pergamon.

Physkon's will was hedged with a reservation. But his illegitimate son, Ptolemy Apion, who ruled in the North African realm of Cyrene, when he died in 96 BC left his kingdom to Rome without qualification. For the first time, a piece of the Ptolemaic inheritance had been deliberately alienated. With usual stealthy footwork, Rome at first stood back a little from this stroke of fortune. For a while, the Greek cities of the kingdom were permitted the luxury of self-government, though Rome took over the royal estates and raised a tax on the medicinal resin known as silphium, the most valuable export product of the land. Then in 74 BC, when all the likely consequences had been argued and judged, and each faction in Rome had considered its own advantage, the decision was made. A quaestor was appointed and the new Roman province of Cyrenaica was brought into being, dangerously poised on the western flank of Egypt.

In 80 BC, with the irony of history, another illegitimate Ptolemy came to the throne, but this time in Egypt itself. Nothos the Bastard, generally known as Ptolemy Auletes, like other weak Ptolemies tossed about by the blows of the Alexandrian mob, placed his faith and his comfort in Rome and clung to the leaders of the Roman factions for support to see him safe amid the savage rivalries of his own homeland. Bribing Romans, he looked as if he would impoverish Alexandrians. He gained the venal friendship of Julius Caesar, but lost Cyprus and his own brother to Marcus Cato without turning a hair. Driven out by corrupt Alexandrians, he was restored by corrupted Romans. Egyptians saw their hateful king contemptuously thrown back to them, and a people that had reason to fear Rome in the past, now had reason for hatred and anger as well.

But what could they do at this late stage? The learned men of the Alexandrian philosophical schools, warned by history and their own timidity, tried hard for a peaceful accommodation with Rome. But the mob and the house of Ptolemy, the one as wilful and foolish as the other, danced together down a riotous, indulgent path to ruin. Their conduct was a lesson in useless depravity, and when much later Dio Chrysostom thought it necessary to lecture the citizens of Alexandria on their many sins, he took the events of Auletes' reign as an example:

> When you managed your own affairs, did not your king play the flute and do little else, while you were his enemies, and made him flee your country to which he was only restored under Roman protection? Then piping and dancing together you destroyed your city.

It was a just accusation.

By then, in 51 BC when Cleopatra came to the throne, the Romans were at the gate, even with a firm foot in the door,

Coin depicting Cleopatra's father, Ptolemy XII.
During his reign Egypt became a client state of Rome.

and were waiting with their usual patience. Carthage had
fallen, Corinth was gone. Macedonia, Armenia, Pontus, Syria
and Cyrene were dust under the Roman sandal. Was there any
reason why Egypt should not follow?

In one respect, Egypt had been fortunate. For nearly a
hundred years, since the tribunate of Tiberius Gracchus in
133 BC, Romans had been so convulsed with the internal strife
of their own state that their foreign affairs had not been a
matter of settled policy but more an adjunct to the ambitions
and rivalries of the great antagonists in Rome. Ever since the
Italian tribes had been overwhelmed and incorporated into
the confederacy of the republic, Rome crept outwards from
Italy, putting faith in conquest. The cohesion of the state at
home almost demanded military adventure abroad. The territory consumed fed the one overriding political concept of the
state, which even in their bitter quarrels gave Romans an
unspoken sense of purpose: Rome was born to rule.

But the question had become, in the years after 133 BC, who
should rule in Rome itself? The state, which had begun with

monarchy and progressed through the free institutions of the republic, went through great circles of contention and grief back to the dictatorship of triumvirs and finally to the imperial despotism of Augustus. Though this was apparently a war of ideals, of democratic forms against patrician autocracy, pitting the people against the senate, the *populares* against the *optimates*, the contest was in fact played out among the coteries of a small number of noble families fighting like rats in a sewer for authority and the spoil that accrued from Roman glory.

As they trod the brutal path to domination, the great faction leaders constantly looked back to Rome, the city of their hopes. They could not afford to do otherwise amid plot and treachery. But to arm themselves for the struggle the participants needed reputation, money and troops, and these were best made and retained abroad. In the reign of Ptolemy Auletes, the triumvirs Crassus, Caesar and Pompey marched tirelessly through the borderlands of the Mediterranean, battering hard Roman roads into Spain, Gaul, Macedonia, Parthia, Syria and other places. But their campaigns were determined by the stresses of the moment, by challenges to Roman authority, and beyond that by individual ambition. The great men carried their conquests to Rome, to claim their triumphs which they waved like flags before their factions, and there was neither time nor agreement for a comprehensive, well-considered policy of conquest in the East.

In these circumstances a country such as Egypt was, with luck, safe from Roman invasion. Egypt had the power and the resources (if not the political will) to make invasion long, arduous and expensive, with no certainty of success. Had not the wild Parthians, barbarians fuelled by raw energy and courage, as recently as 53 BC defeated Crassus at Carrhae with the shameful loss of the legions' eagles?

The land of the Ptolemies was careful not to threaten Roman interests by contentious alliances or ill-advised forays in the East. It paid its dues to Rome in money and deference. Until the internal struggle for power in Rome was resolved, and barring unfortunate entanglements and the quirks of history, Egypt seemed likely to rest in a nervous state of peace.

But with the coming of Cleopatra, feared eventualities began to fall into place. The Roman struggle was entering its last phase, as cunning and treachery picked off the competing champions one by one. That was one blow for Egypt. The other fatal stroke was indeed an entanglement, a fateful meeting of minds and wills and bodies between masters of the Roman world and a young Egyptian queen.

4

CAESAR AND CLEOPATRA

S HE BORE THE NAME of Alexander's sister: Cleopatra, 'glory of the father'. According to the custom of her family she and her co-ruler, her little brother Ptolemy, were the Brother-and-Sister-loving Gods. They were also *Theoi Philopatores*, the Father-loving Gods. Cleopatra knew her place in the successions of her house, her great inheritance stemming from Alexander himself. Her blood was descended from the incest of god-kings with god-queens, and in this mixture who was to say which was the most potent part? The line of Ptolemy was also the line of Arsinoe, a fierce implacable queen, director of her brother-husband's policy, murderer of rivals within and without her family. Yet when she died, older than the king and a tired woman who had left him no children, her husband Ptolemy II Philadelphus mourned her tenderly; she had been the hand in his hand, the consoler of his health, the foundation and brace of his kingdom. Arsinoe was the type of the Ptolemaic queen, and others of the same kind followed after her. Later, in courts of weak men, they knew the art of ruling. They were strong and fearless and without mercy.

Cleopatra VII had it in her bones to be such a queen, and she intended to rule. From her first regnal year, when she was only 18, contrary to Ptolemaic custom the coins of her reign carried her portrait only. It was as if her co-ruler and little brother Ptolemy XIII did not exist. Her coins were clearly stamped *Kleopatras Basilisses* with no other acknowledgement. She wished it to be known that Queen Cleopatra was the ruling monarch of Egypt.

Within a few months of her accession, the sacred bull of Buchis died at the temple of Hermonthis, a few miles from Thebes in Upper Egypt. This white bull, with its coat that seemed to catch and sparkle in the light, contained the terrestrial spirit of the great god Amon-Ra, and the inauguration of a new bull was a deep moment in the religious life of Egypt. The event took place in March 51 BC, and the inscription at the Bucheum recorded that 'the Queen, the Lady of the Two Lands, the Father-loving Goddess, rowed the bull in the barge of Amon to Hermonthis'. Never before, in the meticulous religious records of Egypt, had it been noted that a Ptolemy performed this reverent act in person. It was an astute political statement by the young queen, announcing her identification with the spirit and the life of an older Egypt. She was not just a Macedonian Greek from Alexandria who farmed an alien land for her own benefit from the distant Mediterranean shore. She was an Egyptian whose heart beat in time with the pharaonic tradition, a queen of all her people.

Cleopatra needed whatever help she could get from the body of Egypt, for the scheming at the head, in Alexandria, was as busy as usual. The 10-year-old king, Ptolemy XIII, had been provided with a council of guardians made up of the *dioiketes* Pothinus, a eunuch in charge of finance and administration, the *tropheus* Theodotus, the king's tutor, and the army commander Achillas. Ptolemaic law, regarding co-rulers, had always given kings precedence over queens. If the guardians wished to advance their own ambitions through the manipulation of a child-king, they had a keen interest in limiting and controlling this determined queen. She must be made to see her inferior place.

So her position in the Brucheion palace was full of danger, nor was there any safety in the city beyond. To the habitual wildness of the Alexandrian mob, there was now an added peril from the Roman legionaries, mainly from Gaul and Germany, abandoned in Egypt by Gabinius in 55 BC. Barbarian soldiers trained in the brutal schools of camp and campaign, they were unhinged by the diversions and indulgence of Alexandria. A few years later Julius Caesar found these Gabinians a cause of violent disorder.

> The men of Gabinius [Caesar wrote in the *Civil War*] had grown used to the lax life in Alexandria. Ceasing to think of themselves as Roman and forgetting Roman discipline, they had married and begot children by local wives. And many brigands, pirates, condemned criminals and exiles had joined them. If any were arrested by his master, his comrades would unite to rescue him. A threat to one was a threat to all. So insolent did they become, they demanded the execution of royal favourites, plundered the property of the rich, and besieged the palace for more pay. They dared to try to raise up or pull down kings, as was the ancient Alexandrian tradition.

The Gabinians were a rabble to be feared, but Cleopatra was bold enough to try to limit their destructive influence. When a new Roman proconsul in Syria, Marcus Bibulus,

Votive plaque of Cleopatra as an Egyptian goddess.

ordered the Gabinians to return to his command for the war against Parthia, the rebel troops killed the envoys, who were Bibulus' own two sons. Cleopatra had the murderers arrested immediately and sent to Bibulus in chains. She wished to keep Roman friendship almost at any cost, but it was a brave act for one so insecure to antagonize these riotous brawlers.

For she had other troubles within her realm. In 50 BC the seasonal flood of the Nile had been too low for a good harvest. Drought followed and with it famine. Villages were abandoned and temples grew anxious for their safety. So great was the dearth that Cleopatra was forced to divert resources from the countryside to the vast, consuming metropolis of Alexandria. The decree that ordered this transfer of grain, written in peremptory terms with severe penalties for disobedience, was jointly signed with her brother-king. No doubt she needed to invoke the fullest authority of the Ptolemaic crown and so had to rely on the support of the king's council.

Even then, there were signs that she acted reluctantly or under pressure, for the decree was dated 'in the first year which is also the third year' of the reign. The third year for Cleopatra, but only the first for Ptolemy XIII. Once acknowledged, the king and his council grew in opposition to her sole authority.

Egypt was uneasy for the queen, but there was little comfort either in the world outside. Of the three men, the triumvirs, contending for power in Rome, Crassus was killed at Carrhae in 53 BC. The survivors, Pompey and Caesar, both saw the ultimate prize now within reach. In 49 BC Julius Caesar marched into Italy from Gaul and precipitated civil war. Within a few months Pompey was forced out of Italy. Asia Minor had been Pompey's favourite stamping ground, where his triumphs had been won, and he set out in that direction, pausing first in the Balkans and sending messengers to the East to gather men and money. He sent his most important envoy – his son – to Alexandria, for Egypt was the richest of the eastern lands, and he already possessed there, at least nominally, a formidable if troublesome body of soldiers. The Gabinians, when they were under Roman discipline, had been part of Pompey's faction.

Cleopatra knew that Pompey was not a man to trifle with, and his voice in Rome in the past had been friendly to Egypt. The country still seemed within reach of his powerful arm. So Egypt, whether it was through Cleopatra or the king's council, sent off sixty ships and a large quantity of grain to Pompey's base in Albania. And 500 Gabinians were either bribed or intimidated into rejoining the legions. The rump of the Roman senate that followed Pompey out of Italy passed a resolution of thanks to Egypt and placed Ptolemy XIII under the direct guardianship of Pompey, an equivocal honour for a young Egyptian king, fraught with dangerous consequences for the future.

In Alexandria, the strains of joint rule, made worse by the impending Roman civil war, had destroyed the already fragile harmony within the royal family. Alexandrians had always detested signs of subservience to Rome; the Gabinians resisted the break-up of their lawless community. Pothinus and the council, acting (as Caesar wrote) through the king's 'friends and relatives', fastened the blame on Cleopatra as the senior of the co-rulers and the dominating figure in government. By the end of 49 BC the sentiment of the people of Alexandria had turned against her and she was driven from the capital. Decrees began to be issued in the name of Ptolemy XIII alone.

To drive a Ptolemaic queen from Alexandria was one matter. An angry mob could do that. But to prevent her from plotting a return was much harder. Former Cleopatras, queens of courage and spirit, had proved their ability to foment trouble, to raise armies, and to march back to the city in triumph. Cleopatra IV, in particular, in 113 BC had shown how a queen's revolt might be managed, and Cleopatra VII needed no further encouragement. We read of Cleopatra in Upper Egypt, in the Thebaid, raising an army where the old pharaonic traditions were still strong. Cleopatra well understood her subjects in these lands, as she had shown at the inauguration of the bull of Buchis. Within a year she was ready to move against her brother, and Achillas of the king's council was forced to lead an army to confront her at the north-eastern border near Pelusium.

At this moment, the shadow of Rome suddenly fell dark again on the history of Egypt. In the summer of 48 BC Caesar defeated Pompey at Pharsalus in Thessaly. After this shattering blow Pompey cast around for a means to restore his fortune. He decided to run for Egypt, the land that had helped him before and where the most wealth lay. He was, after all, the self-appointed guardian of the 13-year-old king, who would be unlikely to deny aid to the great Pompey.

In September 48 BC his small fleet approached the Egyptian shore near Mount Casius where the king's forces were drawn up against Cleopatra. A single boat pulled from the beach containing three men of rank – the Egyptian general Achillas, a Roman centurion, and another Roman named Septimius, one of the Gabinian officers. Pompey entered the boat to be rowed ashore. As they closed on the beach Septimius suddenly stabbed Pompey and killed him, and then the Egyptian navy attacked the small number of Roman ships, sinking some and scattering the rest.

It was certain that the murder was planned. Formerly, in the East, Pompey had been the all-conquering general, but now he was merely a fallen hero and a cause for further trouble. In all dealings with Rome, the Ptolemies had always tried to back the winner. Failed men were no longer worth honour or fear. As the king's tutor Theodotus said, 'Dead men don't bite.' Dante, a scathing moralist and keeper of the human conscience, for this act of treachery placed Ptolemy XIII in the same circle of hell as Cain and Judus, since the boy-king had watched the murder from the shore, dressed in the purple *chlamys* of royalty. But the politician and orator Cicero was nearer to the mark when he stated flatly that sooner or later, after Pharsalus, some such end was inevitable for Pompey.

Within a few days the fleet of Julius Caesar, following hard in Pompey's wake, sailed into the Great Harbour of Alexandria with two legions containing more than 3000 foot soldiers and 800 cavalry. Theodotus, the royal tutor and a professor of rhetoric, was the man chosen to offer soft words to the victor of Pharsalus, and he took with him Pompey's signet ring and his severed head. It was both an act of obeisance before the new master of Rome, and a signal that his task was done and that he could go home. It was said that Caesar wept when he saw the head of his enemy. But neither grief nor joy swayed the political calculations of this austere Roman. He had seen too much pain and death to value them beyond their brief moment.

Yet at this crucial instant he did make a mistake. Misreading the psychology of the populace, he decided to overawe the citizens with a full display of Roman pomp. He entered the city in the dress of a consul preceded by lictors bearing the axe and the bundle of rods known as the *fasces*. Intelligent Greeks knew the symbols, and this was seen as an act of possession, which it was. It was too much provocation, as Caesar himself acknowledged in the *Civil War*.

> The multitude considered that this act infringed the king's dignity. The tumult was contained, but for several days there was frequent disturbances by the mob, and a large number of soldiers were killed throughout the city.

Caesar had yet to reach an understanding of the turbulent Alexandrian mentality, nor had he reckoned with the ingrained hostility to Rome. But he was determined not to be driven out until he had made arrangements that were favourable to his own security and to Roman needs. Besides the persuasion of arms, he had several pretexts for being in Egypt. The will of Ptolemy Auletes, lodged in Rome, had placed the king's children and successors under Roman protection. Caesar had also pledged himself to collect the huge debt owed by the Ptolemies to the financier Rabirius. The debt was only half-paid and Caesar, at the end of some ruinously expensive campaigning, badly needed money. He asked immediately for 10 million denarii.

Then he began to dig in, ready to set the discipline of his veteran legionaries against the violence of his unruly opponents. Pothinus, head of the council and spokesman for the Alexandrians, suggested that Caesar should hear the call of his manifold duties in Rome. Caesar was not disconcerted by impertinence. Then Pothinus arranged for musty grain to be delivered to the Roman troops, and had the royal table set with wooden plates and earthenware pots, implying that Romans had stolen the gold and silver vessels. Caesar went steadily on. As guardian of the Egyptian crown, he demanded that the young co-rulers should mend their quarrel and appear before him for reconciliation. Ptolemy XIII left the Egyptian army at Pelusium and made a reluctant visit to the palace of Brucheion with Pothinus to help him.

But Cleopatra faced a problem. She was not unwilling to appear before Caesar. She had already made her case in writing, and this argument was likely to be strengthened (as the historian Dio Cassius noted) by the charm and wit of her person. But she was still camped at the frontier with the army of her brother blocking the way. There was no guarantee of a safe passage to Alexandria. She solved this problem, if a romantic story by Plutarch is to be believed, by a ruse which amply demonstrated that charm and wit:

> She took a small boat manned by her confidant Apollodorus of Sicily and landed near the palace in the dusk. Wondering how to enter undetected, she thought of having herself wrapped in a roll of bedding, which Apollodorus tied up and

carried through the gates to Caesar's apartment. This bold stroke so caught the fancy of Caesar, who admired such daring invention, that he quickly reconciled her to her brother and re-installed them as co-rulers of the kingdom.

Julius Caesar was fifty-two, a man of many struggles already suffering from the headaches and fainting-fits of ill health. He was worn-looking (as the more honest portraits show), with a long lean neck, big nose, the weathered skin of a campaigner, a balding head and large penetrating eyes. His talents and his achievements were extraordinary, as even his greatest enemy would admit. Soldier, scholar, writer, administrator, man of business, politician, visionary statesman, he encompassed whatever he set his hand to. He combined learning with sharp, swift judgement in practical affairs. If he needed it, the winning charm of his personality was as persuasive as his intellect. He was bold in decision, brave in battle, stoical and uncomplaining under hardship, and he was famously popular with his troops whom he led with a subtle mixture of example, iron discipline and genuine sympathy. He

Coin depicting Julius Caesar and dated 42 BC,
two years after his death.

was also vain, ruthless, calculating, often cruel and always driven by his own ambition, though that might be clothed in the dignified garments of principle. His friends felt the warm sun of a great and powerful personality; his enemies courted a sudden death.

Caesar's relations with women were true to his character. He had the power to attract them and the cold deliberation to use them. In the manner of all the noble Roman clans, in their ferocious contest for position and wealth, he had taken on and cast off wives with unseemly haste, with a view to forming political alliances, building factions and gaining funds. He had had many lovers and mistresses, for he seemed to have a strong sexual urge but little potency in the loins since his only offspring was his daughter Julia. Nonetheless it was wise for careful men to hide their pretty women when Caesar was about, as ribald song of his legions proclaimed:

> Home we bring our bald whoremonger.
> Romans lock your wives away.
> All the bags of gold you lent him,
> Went his Gallic tarts to pay!

He liked women, to make love to them and to bring him the broad comforts of humanity that he missed so often pent up in the narrow camp-bed of his many wars. He liked the softness of women, but even more he liked bold scheming females whose intelligence challenged his own and whose wit struck sparks from his own brilliance.

What kind of woman did he see when the surprising bundle was unrolled and the 21-year-old queen of Egypt tumbled out before him? The coins of her reign show various pictures, but all of them were to some degree exercises in state propaganda representing a Ptolemaic ideal. We see, in general, a Cleopatra with a neat, shapely head, wavy hair pulled back into a bun, a determined brow, a generous mouth and a nose rather long and thin. In most portraits the nose is rather hooked. As to her stature and figure and complexion, there is no information.

Ancient prejudice, of which there was plenty, did not seem to include colour prejudice. A person was subject to keen and small-minded criticism for all kind of reasons, from accusations of barbarousness and uncouth speech to superior reflections about the cut of a dress or tunic. But colour was not mentioned. The early Ptolemies were fair-faced Macedonian highlanders, often with a ruddy complexion. They took care to marry within the family. But Egyptian society was mixed, from darkish to quite light skin, with much new African blood being brought in from Nubia and Ethiopia. Mixed marriages were common. And though the Ptolemies married within the family, they were not faithful within the family. The mistresses and concubines of many of the kings were well known. The lovers connected with the successful and long-reigning Ptolemy II were celebrated. There was an Egyptian known by the Greek name Didyme; an actress of vulgar comedies; two girls who were musicians and dancers; Clino who posed naked for popular statues; and Bilistiche, called by Plutarch a barbarian whore from the marketplace, but declared a goddess by her royal lover under the name of Aphrodite Bilistiche. And Ptolmaic queens, women of notorious independence, were as likely to take lovers as their husbands. Who knew the true parentage of many a Ptolemy prince or princess?

The grandmother of Cleopatra was a concubine; her mother is not known for certain. Given all the uncertainties of her ancestry, one scholar has estimated her blood as 32 parts Greek, 27 parts Macedonian and 5 parts Persian. It is a reasonable guess. If she was black, no one mentioned it.

One description of Cleopatra has survived. Although the author, Plutarch, wrote long after Cleopatra's death, his words carry some conviction because his family in the past had been friends with her court doctor.

> Her actual beauty [Plutarch wrote] was not in itself so remarkable; it was the impact of her spirit that was irresistible. The attraction of her person, joined with the charm of her conversation and the characteristic intelligence of all that she said and did, was bewitching. It was a delight merely to hear the sound of her voice. As if this were an instrument of many strings, she could pass from one language to another.

Caesar spoke Greek, as did most educated Romans with an interest in philosophy and literature. Latin was not included in Plutarch's list of Cleopatra's languages. But it is unlikely that a girl talented enough to learn Ethiopian or Arabic, and astute enough to judge the threat to Egypt from Rome, would neglect the rather simple tongue of the masters of the Mediterranean world. Whatever language they used (most probably Greek, as the more subtle and expressive, both for thought and for love), when forceful personality and intelligence met, mediated through the sweetness of their words, each was suddenly revealed to the other.

She was a queen arising out of a famous past, a fabulous history that combined something of the glory of Alexander with the triumphant longevity of Egypt's story. She was the inheritor of a grandiloquence that put to shame such mumbling expressions of the human spirit as he had already seen in

Pontus or Spain or Gaul or even in Italy itself, riches laid down like layers of Nile silt for millennium after millennium.

He was the visionary of Rome, both philosopher and all-conqueror, who seemed to offer at last a chance for peace in a poor warring world now subdued, after the defeat of Pompey, under a great man. At Ephesus, the weary people of the East had recently saluted Caesar as 'Son of Ares and Aphrodite, God made flesh, Saviour of all mankind'.

He was battle-worn, travel-weary, ageing. The ambition of his life was almost within grasp but he knew that the final resolution must take place in Rome. These Alexandrian days were an interlude. He saw a bright but troubled young queen in a tempestuous court surrounded by intrigue, violence and hatred. He could offer her worldly instruction and a strong Roman arm to lean on. Each of them had uses for the other. A startled meeting led to conversation, and respect, and pleasure, and the human instinct for gratified desire, and so to bed. Sex, besides the instant joy, was always a means to an end for worldly and ambitious women, treading delicately in the quicksands of male domination and power. As for Caesar, did not his Julian clan claim descent from Venus, Goddess of Love?

Caesar may have been pleased by the enforced reconciliation he had effected between the young monarchs. But the sulky king, who saw the gains he had made already vanishing in the joint bed of his sister and the Roman, ran lamenting into the street and tore the diadem from his head, to stir up the natural resentment of the Alexandrians against Rome. In this he was helped by Pothinus and Achillas who felt their influence receding as Cleopatra's advanced. The Egyptian army, still gathered near Pelusium, was turned about and led by Achillas back to Alexandria to put the Romans under siege. Caesar had about 4000 men under his command; the

Egyptian army numbered some 20,000 soldiers, including many Gabinians and mercenaries. And the Alexandrian mob was, as ever, ready to turn violence and treachery against the hated foreigners.

All at once Caesar had a difficult little war on his hands. The partial occupation of a large city, hemmed in by a bitter hostility, menaced by street skirmishes and ambushes, was a dangerous task even for a general of Caesar's gifts. Some of his legions were on the march from Syria but time was short. He tried to negotiate with Achillas. But one of his envoys was killed and another severely beaten. He and his Roman veterans were strongly placed for the moment, behind the walls of the royal quarter of Brucheion, bordering the Great Harbour. And with his usual swift reaction Caesar had set fire to the Egyptian warships in the harbour before Ptolemy's men could protect them. Then he stood his ground, as the account of the war partly written by Caesar himself related:

He secured the necessary points and fortified them in the night. From his first arrival Caesar was lodged in a wing of the palace, next door to a theatre that served as a citadel commanding an avenue to the port and other docks. In the next few days he built a rampart in front so he should not be forced to fight against his will.

Since Cleopatra and young Ptolemy were still with Caesar in the palace, he could give the uprising the colour of a rebellion against lawful monarchs. But soon Arsinoe, younger sister of Cleopatra, escaped with the help of a eunuch called Ganymedes. She placed herself at the head of the resistance and raised the standard of legitimate rule against the puppet monarchs under Roman control. This advantage was quickly lost when Arsinoe and Achillas began to quarrel, and when Pothinus was caught sending messages from within the palace to the Alexandrians, Caesar had him executed.

In the street-fighting a fire broke out, perhaps started by the Roman troops to destroy the grain warehouses in the docks. In this conflagration a large store of papyri and book-rolls – Livy says 40,000 volumes – was burnt. Later, it was rumoured, and then believed, that the famous Library itself had been set on fire, as a consequence of Caesar's carelessness. An act like that would have grieved Caesar as much as Alexandria, and the spreading of such a story was as good a way as any to blacken his reputation.

Arsinoe and Achillas continued to quarrel until Arsinoe gained the upper hand. Then she had the army commander arrested and executed. In this place she installed her favourite Ganymedes. The palace eunuch, though only tutor and adviser to the princess, pursued the war with some imagination. He stopped the flow of fresh water from Lake Mareotis into the city's network of canals and waterways, and filled them with salt water instead. Lack of water was a serious blow to the besieged, but Caesar set his men to dig into the harbour beach. With his wide interest in science and topography he had confidence that fresh water would be found there. His men dug anxiously through the night and by morning had reached an adequate spring. With this, they had enough water to hold out, and soon the intense pressure on them was relieved when a fleet of military transports brought the 37th Legion and a good store of supplies.

Into the early months of 47 BC the siege continued with no particular advantage on either side. Then the Roman admiral who had brought in the fleet mounted a swift raid on the island and lighthouse of Pharos and gained control. Caesar followed up immediately, hoping to capture the long mole of the Heptastadion which joined the island to the mainland. The attack faltered. Caesar was outflanked and on the point of being cut off on the mole. His plight unfolded in the impersonal account given in the *Alexandrine War*:

> Caesar, when he saw that they were all giving ground, withdrew to his own boat. He was followed by a crowd who began forcing their way on board, making it impossible to steer the boat or push it off from the land. Sensing what would happen, Caesar jumped overboard and swam to the ships further out. Then he sent small boats to pick up the soldiers in difficulties and thus saved many. As to his own boat, it sank under the weight of numbers, with the loss of all those still on board.

The 52-year-old general, so the story went, swam in armoured breastplate and greaves still holding certain documents above his head 'and would not let them go, though arrows and darts were coming at him and he was often under the water. Still he swam with one hand, holding papers with the other above the water.' Only his purple cloak was left behind for the enemy to claim as a trophy.

At this point, for obscure reasons, Caesar released young king Ptolemy to the Alexandrians. Perhaps Cleopatra worked on her lover to expel the youth. In the confines of a palace under siege, the king, petulantly at odds with his sister, was a liability to morale, and Caesar calculated he had 'nothing to fear from one so young and so ill-prepared for life'. Ptolemy left clutching Caesar's hand and weeping, but once in the city he ordered Arsinoe aside and took command of the Egyptians. Nothing more is heard of the ingenious eunuch Ganymedes.

By March 47 BC the relief force summoned by Caesar from Syria had reached the Egyptian border. The general Mithridates of Pergamon led a mixed army that included 3000 Jewish soldiers under the Idumaean minister Antipater, a presence that persuaded the large Jewish community in Alexandria to back away from Ptolemy. This Roman army stormed Pelusium on the frontier, marched quickly around the apex of the delta, and set off northwards along the western branch of the Nile towards Alexandria. Ptolemy hurried out with the Egyptian army to the corner of Lake Mareotis, hoping to cut off the relief before it could join up with Caesar. But by a night manoeuvre through canals and the lake, Caesar's Romans avoided the Egyptians and joined Mithridates.

In late March a fierce little battle took place. The larger Egyptian army was swept away with merciless efficiency. 'The enemy', said the account in the *Alexandrine War*, 'were so frightened by the attack that they took to their heels, but in vain for few returned to the king.' After a night's pause, the attack was renewed.

Then the Alexandrians struggled to escape and threw themselves over the bank near the river. The first group tumbled into a ditch and were trampled under the feet of the others behind. The king got away in a boat, but so many fugitives crowded aboard that the boat sank and he was drowned.

After the battle, on the same day, Caesar returned to Alexandria by forced march and possessed the city, which for the first time in three hundred years passed entirely into the hands of a foreign general. He was met by Queen Cleopatra, the partner of his days and nights. The subdued citizens received him with 'all those sacred symbols of their religion which they formerly used to appease their angry kings'. Spurred on by the rush of war Caesar was once more his old brisk soldierly self. He ordered a hunt for the body of Ptolemy, for he knew it was necessary to prove his death to this subjects. The drowned body was dredged from the river and the king's golden armour was displayed to the people. Ptolemy XIII was dead; with an astute understanding of Egyptian custom Caesar at once acknowledged the accession of the younger brother Ptolemy XIV to be co-ruler with Cleopatra. Perhaps this was a blow for the queen, who had fought so hard to rid herself of one brother. But she knew that Ptolemaic tradition demanded a co-ruler and her safety in Alexandria depended on it. The city hated her. She had become a good cause for war and defeat, a plaything of the Romans, and an enemy of the independent Greek society that was the glory of Alexandria.

Caesar's Egyptian interlude has been a puzzle. How did it come about that a general of his experience, a master of stratagems and swift action, allowed himself to be caught in the Alexandrian web of deceit and violence? His inferior force, blockaded in a hostile city, was always in danger. With luck and good management Caesar kept the enemy at bay, but he could not defeat it until reinforcements arrived. At any moment, he might have been swept away. Caesar's own explanation for this state of misery lacked conviction. He said he had been detained against his will 'by the Etesian winds which blow into the harbour and make exit difficult'. The judgement of others was that infatuation, not contrary winds, held him back. Who can doubt that Cleopatra had much to do with it, but she was only part of the pattern not the whole picture.

Caesar had permitted himself a moment of relaxation. After years of upward struggle he saw the summit ahead,

clearly lit and accessible. He paused for breath, and his grip
slipped a little. Some lack of attention, a judgement of men
and places that was less keen than usual had jammed him into
a corner of Alexandria under siege. But for a man used to
extremities of danger, his position was not really *serious*. He
had a body of well-trained veterans solidly established behind
good fortifications. He had access to the Great Harbour and
from there, with difficulty, to the sea. He was faced by a large
number of angry but ill-disciplined opponents, poorly led and
themselves hampered by the tight constraints of street warfare. His admiral Euphranor had brought supplies and extra
troops. His loyal general Mithridates would be bringing an
army from Syria as soon as possible. And in the meantime, as
he sat out this awkward impasse, there were compensations.

He had met a young woman of a kind he had never seen
before. He had kissed and left many a girl in many places.
Powerful Roman ladies, talented women who pursued dynastic ambition with all the deadly strength of men, had won his
respect and even his affection. But when he gave Servilia, that
brooding mistress of Roman politics, jewels said to be worth a
million denarii, had he ever such a return as from this slip of
an Egyptian queen? Such conversation, such a delightful clash
of ideas, so much learning and sparks of wit, flirtations, the
tricks of love, profound moments and then the retreat into
each other's arms. And where else but in this court in the
shade of the Museum and Library could he recover the
memory of Alexander the Great, the exemplar of his hopes?
Here, too, he could talk of Thales and Plato, of Euripedes and
Aristophanes. He could see the manuscripts of Theocritus and
other great poets, and best of all of mighty Homer himself
whose extant writings lay on the shelves of this very Library.
And when the scholarly talk was done, there were still feasts

and entertainments and drolleries and music and dance to put to shame staid Rome with its vulgar triumphs and blundering excesses. 'His greatest favourite was Cleopatra', wrote Suetonius, 'with whom he would often revel all night till the dawn of day.'

He knew these times must end. After the victory over Ptolemy and the settling of Egyptian affairs, Caesar was anxious to get away. But before he went, Cleopatra arranged for him one last elegaic celebration to remind of all that he had gained, and all that he stood to lose, now that he was about to take up the interrupted business of his life. She took him sailing far up the Nile in the Egyptian royal barge, a vessel nearly 100-metres long of unexampled luxury, with audience chambers to catch the breath and private withdrawing-rooms to make the senses reel, with viewing platforms and canopied sun-decks, and even a temple or two. They would have gone as far south as the Ethiopian border had not Caesar's army refused to follow. The soldiers were desperate for home and Caesar went with them.

He left at the beginning of the summer. Egypt was nominally in the hands of the co-rulers Cleopatra and Ptolemy XIV, the brother ten years her junior. But three legions under the freedman Rufinus remained in Egypt with orders to keep a careful watch, 'to support the monarchs', said the *Alexandrine War* 'who had neither the affection of their own people, because they had been loyal to Caesar, nor the authority of long usage, because they had ruled jointly for only a few days'. Then the writer added ominously that 'if the rulers of Egypt remained loyal, they would have our protection, but if ungrateful, then these same soldiers would punish them'.

Rufinus and his legions were warning enough to the Egyptian people. But in case the message was still not clear, Caesar also took with his departing army Cleopatra's disgraced sister Arsinoe, to walk in chains in his Roman triumph. He left behind the queen pregnant with his child.

Cleopatra's baby was born on Payni 23 (23 June) 47 BC. The little boy was declared to be the son of the Roman general and named Caesar, though he was always known by the diminutive Caesarion. It was a provocative act in Rome-hating Alexandria to proclaim openly this bastard child. But Alexandria was for the moment lost to Cleopatra and was only kept peaceful by Rufinus and the legions. Cleopatra's strength, and the mark of her intelligent reading of Egyptian history, lay not in her own Greek-speaking capital but in her appeal to the great mass of the native people beyond. The first formal act of her reign had been a solemn visit to Upper Egypt on an occasion of religious importance. The recent pleasure-journey with Caesar up the Nile, though light-hearted in almost all respects, was still a visitation by a monarch to her subjects, to show the nature of majesty and the bond between queen and people.

So the event that enraged Alexandria was celebrated near Thebes. An inscription at Hermonthis welcomed the baby as the child of Amon-Ra created through the human agency of Julius Caesar. The day of birth was declared a feast of Isis, and a coin struck in Cyprus (ceded back to Egypt's queen by her Roman lover) showed Cleopatra as Isis-Aphrodite suckling Caesarion as the infant god Horus-Eros.

Once Caesar was free of Egypt he seemed determined to make up for the indulgence of his days in Alexandria. He swept across Asia Minor, brushing aside Pharnaces of Pontus with such ease that he recalled an old Greek tag and boasted, 'I came, I saw, I conquered.' In September he was back in Italy but was drawn away again to face one of the last despairing uprisings of Pompey's followers in North Africa. In April 46 BC he defeated them at Thapsus and had returned to Rome by the end of July. Now he could attend to the propaganda of his great achievements and delight the fickle Roman population with no less than four triumphs celebrating his conquests in Gaul, Egypt, Pontus and North Africa.

Here was heaven-sent opportunity for political show and Caesar made the most of it, particularly in the triumph over Egypt. The colossus of the ancient world was brought low, and as a sign of subjugation – amid the statue of the Nile-god, the giant model of light-flashing Pharos, and lurid representations of the deaths of Pothinus and Achillas – the dejected figure of Arsinoe walked in chains, the greatest princess ever to face the humiliation of a Roman triumph. The usual brutal custom had been to kill the captives after the show, but Caesar, out of humanity or some other compunction, spared her life.

At one moment, in the triumphal processions, coarse soldiers and the underlings of Rome had been bawling ribald songs of the general's amours, of fumblings in oriental courts with a queen of exotic splendour. Then suddenly that queen herself was in Rome, with her brother-husband and all her strange retinue. Cleopatra and Ptolemy XIV, so uneasy in Alexandria, had come to tie even closer the bond with Rome and to solicit official confirmation of *amicitia* from the senate and the people. Caesar was now so completely in control of the Roman state that the recognition of the Egyptian co-rulers as Rome's 'friends and allies' was easily granted.

But beyond any business of state, Cleopatra had come to Rome for the sake of Caesar. They were no longer constant lovers. Malicious mouths in the town reported that he had passed on to Eunoe, wife of King Bogud of Mauretania. But the intimacy of sex had sealed a political and human affiliation between Caesar and Cleopatra. Caesar did not repudiate the past, nor did he deny the paternity of the baby who bore his name. Rather, he paid Cleopatra as great an honour as was within his power. In the new Forum Julium, constructed by Caesar at huge expense as an annex to the Forum Romanum, beside the cult-statue of Venus Genetrix, the goddess celebrated as Mother and Founder of the Julian clan, he placed a gilded statue of Cleopatra.

No compulsion forced him to do this. His legions already controlled Lower Egypt. A place in his bed was now given to another, and he had no wish to marry Cleopatra for dynastic or political purposes. Calpurnia was Caesar's wife, and Roman law did not permit either bigamy or a marriage between a patrician and a foreigner. It was thought possible that Caesar had been so infected by the humours of the Ptolemaic court during this close days with Cleopatra that he was no longer content to be just the dictator of the Roman state. Perhaps he aspired to the deification of his person, to become god-king as the Ptolemies claimed to be? The introduction of the goddess-queen Cleopatra into the shrine of Caesar's clan seemed an ominous sign to republican opponents. When would the dictator follow the queen into the temple? In May 45 BC the senate was persuaded to erect in the temple of Quirinus a statue of Julius Caesar bearing the inscription 'To the Unconquered God'. Quirinus was the deified Romulus, the founder of Rome who later became its tyrant, and for this, so it was said, he was torn in pieces. 'I had rather', Cicero wrote with bitter irony, 'he were a companion in the temple of Quirinus than of Salus.' Better that he show his true colours as a tyrant than masquerade as the friend of Safety. The daggers of assassination were beginning to be sharpened.

Some time late in 46 BC Cleopatra and her court settled into a large villa on Caesar's estate just across the Tiber, under the slope of the Janiculum hill. In these peaceful surroundings, amid gardens and country breezes but within easy reach of the political heart of Rome, she began to test Rome society. Her notoriety, both as Egypt's queen and as Caesar's mistress and mother of his son, guaranteed the attendance of the curious and the fashionable. The force of her personality, her strong sense of politics and her ability still to influence Caesar pulled sober senators again and again to her door, some with respect and some in horrified fascination.

Under her influence, leaning on the tradition of scholarship, culture and invention that she brought from Alexandria, Caesar set afoot several ambitious plans for improvement and reform. In imitation of the Alexandrian Library, Terentius Varro, a man of many bright talents who had fought against but been pardoned by Caesar, began the task of bringing together a collection of all Greek and Roman literature. In Alexandria, too, Caesar had seen the Egyptian-Greek skill in hydraulic engineering, and he now proposed a scheme for a canal that would drain the malarial swamp of the Pontine marshes and link the Tiber to Terracina. Even more important was the work on the reform of the calender undertaken on Caesar's orders by the mathematician Sosigenes from the Museum in Alexandria. The lunar year used in Rome had grown seriously out of step with the astronomical year and required a large correction. A new solar year, based on calculations that Sosigenes had drawn from Ptolemaic astronomy, was successfully introduced on 1 January 45 BC. This reform was called the Julian calendar in honour of Caesar; with more justice it might have been called after Cleopatra and her Alexandrian scientist.

These were virtuous plans for the benefit of society. Much more doubtful and dangerous in Roman eyes was the introduction of the cult of Dionysus, formerly banned in Rome. The eastern god of mystery and excess, so attractive to the Alexandrians, concentrated all the vague fears and nameless horrors that Romans identified with Egyptian life. Surely Cleopatra had brought this monstrous god with her. Now Rome began to see deceit, frenzy, riot, irrational violence slowly darken habitual Roman clarity.

But no Ptolemaic court could exist for long without its pleasures, and even in Rome, where crudity vied with prudery, Cleopatra would not forego the delights of art and entertainment. Tigellius Hermogenes, famously delicate and demanding, sang for her. The philosopher Philostratus laid out his rhetorical flourishes for a select company. Aristocrats of the beau monde flocked to her bold feasts and discreet dinners. She met the large cast of idealists and opportunists gathered for the acting out the Roman drama. Was it tragedy or comedy? Mark Antony was there, and though Cleopatra had seen him when she was a girl in Alexandria she might not have met him now, for he was temporarily out of favour with Caesar. But Cicero, the shrewd observer, the distressed republican who admired Caesar but loved Rome more, could not keep away. He was drawn not just by curiosity but also by the easy assembly of cultured minds whose learning matched his own. For the queen herself, he could hardly suppress a shudder. Her divinity and the ruthless autocracy of the Ptolemaic state went against all his beliefs. But a little exchange of manuscripts or beautiful objects between discriminating scholars was not something to reject. Nor should such pleasantries be considered a bribe, rife though bribery was in this sorry world. 'They are quite consistent with my position', he wrote indignantly; 'I would not hesitate to declare them in the public assembly.' Yet when Cicero came to a final judgement, after Caesar's death, his stoic and republican heart could not approve of Cleopatra.

> I hate the queen [he wrote in a letter to a friend]. When she lived in the gardens across the Tiber, I cannot speak of her arrogance without pain. I will have nothing to do with these people. They give me no credit for spirit nor even for a capacity of resentment.

Resentment he certainly had, and so too did a large part of the Roman populace.

For Cleopatra had become fully identified with Caesar's own aims, for which she was partly blamed. These aims were feared by very many. If not a goddess to the Romans, Cleopatra was at least a sorceress, a weaver of strange, self-deluding spells that ensnared a simple Roman virtue. Caesar was now well-launched on the slope to imperial, even god-like, authority. His best intentions were misconstrued in the poisoned atmosphere. After the reform of the calendar, when someone mentioned to Cicero the expected rise of a certain constellation, he replied tartly, 'Yes, by edict!' Caesar's radical changes in the senate were seen as skulduggery and factional packing. 'Here's a good idea', cried graffiti on a wall. 'Don't show the new senators the way to the senate-building!' Caesar was no longer open to argument, and dictatorial pride had made him remote and haughty. When a group from the senate came humbly to offer him his own temple, dedicated to Divus Julius, he did not even rise to greet the delegation.

The pressure of ambition and a vast burden of work prevented Caesar from spending much time with Cleopatra. He was not much seen in the gardens of the Janiculum. His health, uncertain for some time, was growing worse – crushing headaches, faints, epileptic fits. At the end of 46 BC a revolt using Pompey's well-remembered name dragged him to Spain. He returned victorious in the summer of 45 BC, but badly in need of rest and convalescence. He retired to his estates south of Rome, and there he made his will which he deposited, as was customary, with the Vestal Virgins.

In his absence the rumourmongers had been silent about Cleopatra. Perhaps she also had been away, even to Egypt to foster and protect the source of her power. By the time Caesar was ready to return to Rome, in October 45 BC, she was back there too, and once more she was the subject of malicious tongues. It was said that Caesar planned to move his capital from Rome to Alexandria. And he would marry the oriental witch skulking across the Tiber. The tribune Cinna, according to a tale reported later by the historian Suetonius, had drawn up a decree on Caesar's instruction 'making it lawful for Caesar to marry as many wives as he wished'.

Julius Caesar, it seemed to Rome, had the world in his hand, to deal with it as insolently as he saw fit. In February 44 BC, at the feast of Lupercalia, he sat in the Capitol on a golden throne and received from Antony the title and the diadem of a king. Despite the acclamation of his claque, the crowd watched in silence and only broke into a thunder of applause when he took off the diadem and handed it back. He should have been warned, and especially so when the Sibylline Books were opened and declared that the projected war against Parthia could only be won by a king. There were some things that a true Roman, even a partisan of Caesar, could not stomach, and one of these was a blatant, open assumption of a king's name.

The plans for the campaign against Parthia were well advanced. This war would avenge the defeat and death of Crassus, and the loss of the Roman eagles, nine years before. It would also be the last step in Caesar's regal progress, and confirm him in his imperium, his mastery of the world.

Caesar was set to leave on 17 March 44 BC. Since the departing general, who was no longer her lover but her soul-mate and confidant, was likely to be away for some time, Cleopatra also made preparation to go. Egypt needed her, and she needed her own country. She and Caesar had given one another what each desired. Their fateful meeting, though leading her to full, passionate womanhood, had enmeshed her in the destiny of Rome. And for him, the self-contained Roman schemer, what did he see beyond the joys of an ardent woman? Perhaps she made him dream on delusions of divinity and authority such as he had seen obscurely in the Greek world-hero Alexander and practically in the long rule of that great man's Ptolemaic successors. In any case, the Egyptian queen and the Roman dictator were done with each other now, and they could depart in peace.

On the Ides of March, 15 March 44 BC, the swords of the conspirators brought Caesar's dream to an abrupt end.

5

BREATHING SPACE

THE MOMENT WAS PERILOUS. Caesar's death cancelled expectations and made guesswork of certainty. Should the Egyptian queen stay or run? Cleopatra had never lacked nerve. She drew on her store of courage and waited a little. The reading of Caesar's will gave her no comfort. After bequeathing his gardens on the Tiber to the people and giving each Roman 300 sestercii, gifts that wrung tears from the populace, Caesar did not mention Caesarion, his bastard son, but made his great-nephew Octavius the adopted successor and spiritual heir to whom he gave three-quarters of his estates.

In the chaos of the time, when the consul Antony played on the senate and the conspirators with such skill and diplomacy, the name of Cleopatra flickered through the pages of Cicero's correspondence. Cicero was implicated by his sympathies and his meddling and he was desperate to catch the drift of events. A month after the murder he wrote, 'I see nothing to object to in the flight of the queen.' But in the second week in May she was still in Rome, the subject of further rumours to which

Cicero obscurely referred: 'I'm hoping it is true about the queen and that Caesar.' Later writers, in particular the loose-mouthed poet Lucan commenting a century afterwards, suggested that Cleopatra was kept in Rome by a miscarriage of another baby whose father was also Caesar. But on 17 May Cicero noted that 'the rumour about the queen is dying down', and a week later added, 'I am hoping it is true about the queen.' Without doubt Cicero was hoping for bad news about Cleopatra. He did not like Greeks and he did not like women, and most of all he hated the Greek woman Cleopatra, as he admitted to his friend Atticus on 17 June. The misogynist Cicero is a poor witness against Cleopatra, but his political judgement was still keenly attuned to the Roman turmoil.

> Now I see it was folly [he wrote on 24 May] to be consoled by the Ides of March. Our courage was that of men but, believe me, we had no more sense than children. We have only chopped down the tree, not rooted it up.

Nothing was settled by Caesar's murder. The Roman contest began again, a new struggle in which Cleopatra for the moment had no place. The sensible road for her led back to the homeland. She had been preparing for it before Caesar's death, and now she went.

In trying to protect herself and the Egyptian monarchy by going to Rome, Cleopatra had been neglecting Egypt itself. When she returned, there was much work to do. Once again, for two consecutive years, the Nile flood had fallen below the measures known as 'the cubits of death' and hardship and some famine followed, as they always did from these periodic disasters. And once again calamity laid bare the latent tensions within the state, the tug-of-war between the productive native

Cleopatra's cartouche showing the queen's name
spelt in hieroglyphic signs.

countryside and the huge consuming metropolis, between the
lean forgotten south and the pampered sybarites of Alexandria. A stele put up at about this time by the priests of Amon-
Ra at Thebes, in honour of the chief magistrate of their
district, lamented the state of their region 'ruined by a variety
of grievous circumstances'. The people of Thebes praised
their magistrate, Callimachus, for his heartfelt care in the
recent times of famine and pestilence, and commended his
attachment to old ways and old faith. No credit was given to
the reigning monarchs, who were not mentioned in the
inscription, except in the dating by the years of the reign.

Disease followed famine. With the impartial curiosity of
Alexandrian science, Dioscurides Phacas, a man known as
Freckles, tracked the spread of the pestilence. He noted the
distended black blotches and the suppurations from lymphatic

glands, and in doing so described for the first time the symptoms and the course of the bubonic plague.

To address the troubles of the kingdom required from the queen a most delicate balance. To some degree, the rights and duties of the regions in such a large diverse land were irreconcilable. But agriculture was of the first importance, and Cleopatra was forced to make some hard decisions in the apportionment of labour and produce. In the emergency, she made a distribution from the royal granaries from which the large Jewish community in the Delta quarter of Alexandria was excluded. The law placed the Jews, as foreigners, outside the largesse of the state, even though the community had been established for generations. Cleopatra can hardly have hesitated between her own people and foreigners, but her decision won her an enduring Jewish enmity. Much more difficult were the judgements that had to be made between the groups of her own subjects, as a decree from Heracleopolis, dated April 41 BC, showed. In the face of shortages local administrators in the countryside were placing extra burdens and dues on Alexandrians who did agricultural work outside the city. The queen declared herself to be 'exceedingly indignant' and ordered that no excessive demands should be made on these workers.

> Nor shall their goods be destrained for such contributions, nor shall any new tax be required of them, but when they have once paid the essential dues, in kind or in money, for corn-land and for vine-land, which have regularly in the past been assigned to the royal treasury, they shall not be molested for anything further, on any pretext whatsoever.

Slowly, some of the neglect of agriculture was put right and production began to increase. As a promise of a new age of plenty Cleopatra, as ever the adept propagandist, placed on the reverse of her coins the double cornucopia and the fillet of the royal diadem formerly used by her predecessor Arsinoe II, the queen remembered as the Lady of Abundance.

The plight of agriculture had called for emergency measures. The other business to which Cleopatra gave immediate attention was in fact the enduring preoccupation of her reign: to secure her own position, and even more the future of her dynasty, by all the means that intrigue, politics and religion allowed. Very soon after her return to Egypt her brother-husband Ptolemy XIV was heard of no more. Later writers, in particular the unfriendly Jewish historian Josephus, stated the young king had been poisoned. It would be no surprise if Cleopatra killed the youth. Murder within the family was a hazard of Ptolemaic rule. Cleopatra had fought her other brother-husband Ptolemy XIII to a bitter end, seeing without grief his drowned body brought to Alexandria by Caesar's soldiers. She did not forgive her sister Arsinoe for her flight from the palace, when the young girl had gone over to Pothinus and Achillas. When the chance came, a few years later, for Cleopatra to rid herself of Arsinoe, she demanded her sister's execution without hesitation. Ptolemy XIV was an impediment, for he held a position that she had daringly marked for another. The practice of the Egyptian monarchy, which required a co-ruler for a queen, had raised Ptolemy XIV to the kingship. But he was a mere cipher, as easily cast down as raised up. The plan she had now formed swept her brother away and replaced him with three-year-old Caesarion, her son by Julius Caesar.

To Egyptians, the marriage within the crown of a mother and her infant son was a formal trifle, easily swallowed. More difficult to take was the illegitimacy of the child, though he was at least clearly within the Ptolemaic line through his mother. The sticking-point, the offence that caught in the throats of Alexandrians especially, was the Roman father of this newly crowned Ptolemy Caesar. But for Cleopatra, the decision, though boldly provocative, was logical enough. She thought that Caesar's child was the best counter she had to defend herself against any further Roman designs on Egypt. She gambled that the elevation of a half-Roman to be co-ruler of Egypt already brought the kingdom within the orbit of the Roman imperium. With Ptolemy Caesar – Caesarion – in place, Rome would need no greater presence in Egypt. Cleopatra had always understood that she needed Romans to save her country from Rome. What better, then, than a half-Roman co-ruler who was also her little son?

Alexandrians would choke on this offering, as Cleopatra very well knew. With them, she was prepared to brazen it out. She had defied them before and would do so again. It was of much more importance to her to have the new arrangement confirmed and accepted within the wide boundaries of her realm. For the future of her dynasty Ptolemy Caesar had to be seen as a king in the Egyptian tradition, a true successor in the long line of the pharaohs.

The shrewd propaganda of the queen had already proclaimed the divine provenance of her child. In the ancient Egyptian practice, stories in pictures were put on temple walls to illustrate the descent of a new-born royal child from Amon-Pharaoh through his Isis-Queen. 'These pictures', writes one sympathetic scholar, 'reproduced not merely a dogma, namely the teaching about the divine birth of Pharaoh, but also a sacred ritual drama.' This was the tradition that Cleopatra deliberately followed. In the celebratory inscription for the birth of Caesarion at Hermonthis in Upper

Egypt, the meaning of the event is bluntly underscored by doing away with the usual symbols of queen-as-goddess and child-as-god and plainly showing these deities in their human figures.

> Cleopatra is shown kneeling, attended by goddesses, and above her is her new name *Mother of Ra* in hieroglyphs. Over the new-born child stands the device of the scarab, marking out the young Ptolemy Caesar as God of the Rising Sun.

In another scene two babies – Horus and Caesarion – are suckled on a couch by goddesses with the heads of cows, while Amon and Mut and Cleopatra herself lend a divine lustre to the nursing of the babe.

This tale of divine birth was the fable that she also propagated when she had placed on her coins the figure of herself as Isis suckling Caesarion in the guise of Horus. But now, with her son assimilated into the divine kingship, she needed to give her people further instruction, although they had shown that they were already familiar with her insistent message. A stele inscribed in the Fayum soon after her return from Rome made a dedication to the crocodile-god on behalf of Queen Cleopatra and King Ptolemy Caesar, who were declared jointly to be the great-grandchildren of the god. But some more resplendent gesture was needed, some star-burst of affirmation of the co-rulers' divine role, and this was provided at about this time on the wall of the temple of Denderah in Upper Egypt (see Plate 11).

The symbolic representation, in huge figures, was both grand and subtle. Here, in colossal relief, stand Queen Cleopatra and in front of her a full-scale male named as Ptolemy Caesar. They bear gifts of musical instruments and gold which they are offering to Hathor, one of the goddesses of the temple and the goddess of music and love. She was the Egyptian equivalent of Aphrodite and therefore the appropriate deity to receive gifts from love's servant Cleopatra and her love-child Caesarion.

But that was not the whole story, as the skill of Egyptologists has revealed. The noble figure standing in front of Ptolemy Caesar is Isis, the goddess who is the sister-wife of Osiris, and one already identified with the queen in the mythology of the royal birth. Isis is the consort and saviour of Osiris, who brings the slaughtered god back to life and is then delivered of his divine child. The son born to them is the god Horus, the Sun God of Egypt, the God who united the Two Lands, and thus the archetype of each new-born pharaoh who would also rule in Upper and Lower Egypt. The holy message, therefore, to be read on the wall of Denderah was as follows: Isis-Cleopatra had conceived out of the dead god Osiris-Caesar (for had not the Romans in a fit of guilt deified Julius Caesar also?), and the child of their union was Horus-Caesarion, now properly called Ptolemy Caesar, the divinely appointed co-ruler of the Two Lands of Egypt. And this was the king destined in the future (if he realized his mother's magnificent dream) to reconcile under one crown the two empires of Egypt and Rome.

To those untrained in the arcana of Egyptian religious symbolism the message on the wall of Denderah might seem grotesque and far-fetched. But the Egyptian priesthood had studied the interpretation of pictures and hieroglyphs for millennia, and they read the symbolic meaning quite easily. Then the priests remembered the commitment of the queen to themselves, their temples and the traditions of their faith. They were able to see on the stele at the Bucheum at

Hermonthis that Cleopatra, for the glory of the sacred bull, had given 412 silver pieces for a table of offerings, a daily allowance of bread, wine and milk for the priestly staff, and 27 measures of oil for the performance of the daily rites. And for the general support of the shrine and its workers she also paid for meat, beans and oil. They saw also that under her administration the grants made to the temples for the exercise of religious functions – the *syntaxis* – were kept up. They noted that her dangerous intimacy with Rome seemed, at least for the time being, to keep the land safe from Roman invasion. Forgiving her those very failings for which the Alexandrians held her in contempt, the priests recognized her as their native goddess-queen. They understood the message she had so gigantically engraved at Denderah, and they passed it on to their vast, illiterate, faithful flock among the Egyptian peasantry.

For a bright moment it looked as if Cleopatra might have succeeded in her plans to secure both her own present and her son's future. Conditions in Egypt were slowly improving, though they were still dire enough in places to force free men and women to sell themselves into servitude. Despite the economic troubles, the queen was building a new fleet and restocking the royal granaries. The Roman legions left behind by Caesar had subdued the hostile Alexandrians into a surly obedience. But she could not divorce herself and her kingdom from the course of history that was being shaped in Rome.

On the death of Caesar, his heir designate Octavius, a pale, slight, sickly youth of eighteen, returned from military training in Apollonia and after a time took on the name of his adoptive father, though in this period of his life he became known to history as Octavian. The firmness of his decision and the steady determination to avenge his great-uncle's murder belied his youth and his weak constitution and showed something of the qualities that Caesar had noted in him when they were together in Spain in the previous year. Despite early lack of support and many setbacks Octavian clung to his conviction. In July, in the depressed and muddled months after the murder, when he insisted on celebrating the Ludi Victoriae Caesaris – the triumph for Caesar's victory at Thapsus – despite opposition, a comet appeared in the sky, which was taken by both Octavian and the populace as the welcome of the gods for the divine Caesar. Octavian knew then that his path was marked out and he never wavered.

In the days after the murder the consul Antony averted worse disaster with fair speech and the skill of his diplomacy. He set himself as the standard-bearer of Caesar's following, but the forces for disorder pulled too strongly for him to control for long. He formed an uneasy alliance with Octavian to whom he referred with condescension as 'the boy who owed everything to a name'. The two were as far apart in character as mountain and sea. But the name Octavian had assumed was the great name of the dead man, and this was the most potent rallying-call to all those, particularly the soldiers of the legions, who had reason to remember Caesar's extraordinary accomplishments.

In the summer of 44 BC the leaders of the assassins, Brutus and Cassius, abandoned Italy for Asia Minor where they hoped to raise men and money for the inevitable contest. In Rome, relations between Antony and Octavian were wearing thin. Cicero began to attack Antony in the senate in the famous series of speeches known as *Philippics*, while Antony, to weaken Octavian's position, declared before the senate that Caesar had recognized Caesarion as his son. Caesar's party split. Amid accusations and plots and much deceitful jostling, the split widened into open warfare. The senate ordered

Octavian to join the consuls for the new year 43 BC in an attack on Antony. The opponents met at the battle of Mutina in April 43 BC. Antony was defeated and driven into Gaul, both consuls fell on the field of battle, and Octavian was left in sole command of Rome. As the victorious general he swept into the city and took the vacant consulship by intimidation. From this position of vantage he began to stitch together the torn fabric of Caesar's party, for he knew that the immediate contest was not with Antony but with the murderers gathering their forces in the East.

In October, Octavian went to Bononia to meet Antony and Lepidus, the soldier who had succeeded Antony as Caesar's master of horse. In formal harmony that hid their inner feelings these three men joined together in the Second Triumvirate for 'the re-organization of the Roman State'. They issued a proscription list of those they deemed to be implicated in the death of Caesar. Three hundred senators and no less than 3000 men of the rank of *equites* forfeited life and property to the state, and now the triumvirs had the money to pursue an eastern war against Brutus and Cassius.

From the safety of Egypt, Cleopatra watched these events with cautious concern. She was naturally of Caesar's party, but her instinct warned her very strongly not to get involved with the internal struggles of the Roman state. In Syria, the republican Cassius was being opposed by Caesar's loyal general Dolabella. Cleopatra permitted or connived at the departure of the legions still in Egypt to go to the help of Dolabella. But in July 43 BC, when Dolabella was surrounded and committed suicide at Laodicea, these legions went over to Cassius. At this time also, the Egyptian governor of Cyprus supported Cassius, with the implicit approval of Arsinoe, Cleopatra's unlucky sister who had walked in Caesar's triumph and then been banished to the temple of Artemis in Ephesus. Cypriot ships defected to Cassius and the Ephesians saluted Arsinoe as queen of Egypt.

It seemed that Cassius had carried all before him along the eastern shore of the Mediterranean and his army was dangerously close to Egypt. All the princes of the region had submitted to the republican general, except in Egypt where Cleopatra was still studiously non-committal. Cassius, as eager as all others for Egyptian wealth, was on the point of changing her mind by invasion when an urgent call from Brutus summoned him to Smyrna to prepare to meet the advance of the triumvirs.

If Cleopatra was not ready to support Cassius, she was also in some doubt about Octavian. He, merely a great-nephew, had stolen the birthright that might have gone to her son Caesarion. But she saw that some resolution was approaching and it was time for her to indicate some preference. Despite her suspicion of him, Octavian had shown no predatory interest in Egypt and he was still far away. She knew Antony as Caesar's friend and admirer, and her sympathies lay with his faction. When Cassius had asked Cleopatra for aid, she had fended him off with a plea of poverty, owing to disease and famine in the kingdom. But suddenly she put to sea with her own fleet, commanding it herself with an imperial grandeur unprecedented in a queen, heading for the Adriatic with help and supplies for the triumvirs. But after a short passage, the display of armed might turned to farce as gales tore the fleet apart and a bedraggled queen, green with sea-sickness, limped back to the Great Harbour in Alexandria. She was getting together another fleet when news came, in the autumn of 42 BC, that Brutus and Cassius had been defeated and killed at Philippi, and with them perished also the republican cause in Rome.

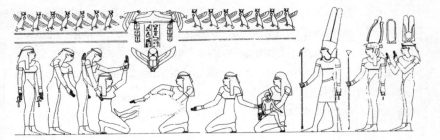

Stela depicting the birth of the child-god Harpocrates before
the eyes of Amun-Re, the goddess Nechbet and Cleopatra.
The winged scarab above the child (partly damaged)
symbolizes the King of Upper and Lower Egypt.

The Roman world had fallen to the triumvirs. The only
obstacles now standing in their way were the resistance that
Pompey's son Sextus was stirring up in Sicily and the contrary
pulls of their own ambitions. After some sparring the empire
was divided between the three men. Italy was declared to be
common ground for all of them. Lepidus, who was suspected
of an agreement with young Pompey, was promised North
Africa once he had cleared his name. Octavian took Spain and
Sardinia but continued to be based in Rome. Antony, the general of the victory at Philippi, took what seemed to be the
lion's share. Transalpine Gaul fell to him and all the eastern
possessions of the empire, where he accepted the task of settling the legions and raising the money for the long-delayed
conquest of Parthia.

In Rome, Antony now appeared to be first among men; but
the contradictions of his brawling, easy-going, pleasure-loving
character fated him always to fall under the shadow of
another's superior resolution. He was brilliant at many things,
but he lacked the single-minded application to turn talent into

achievement. He was a dashing, forceful cavalry commander, but too brash and careless for the gritty perseverance needed in a good general. He might win a battle but less easily a campaign. He was a persuasive orator, a philhellene, a quick mind with sharp instincts and good understanding. He was affable and warm-hearted and often generous to his enemies. It was Antony who had covered dead Brutus with his cloak at Philippi, to prevent the dreadful butcheries that Octavian wished to inflict on the body. But in other cases Antony, too, was capable of that unfeeling Roman cruelty.

In the conduct of state business, Antony could charm and beguile important men, and he could thump the table in the rough camaraderie of the camp, drinking the night away with his sweat-stained troops. He had the cunning for sudden stratagems, but not the craft for the long tedious pull of a political campaign. He loved drink and women, and abused them both in the name of good fellowship, but it is a matter of doubt who finally was the master, love or Antony. He was ambitious, but even ambition – that deadly serious part of a great Roman's *gravitas* – could not keep his attention. His mind wandered – women, food, drink, prowess at arms, mighty deeds, jokes, entertainments, convivial company, sleep, and then another sun-filled day to keep him amused. Perhaps he could not teach himself to care enough for world and reputation. What came easily he would take, but he would not pay the price for the hard accomplishments.

Antony was about forty when history offered him the chance of greatness, a big burly bear of a man with wild curls. In rude good health, he modelled himself perhaps too consciously on Heracles, a short tunic tucked up on his rump to show thunderous legs, a large brutal sword on his hip. One look at him said he was a mighty drinker, a roisterer with an unpredictable, invincible, magnanimous spirit. And there was much in his early life to confirm this view of himself. Careless in everything, he threw around his money, his abilities, his reputation and his heart. Many in Rome, both the virtuous and the mean-minded, abhorred him. Cicero, in whom a censorious, pinched spirit always contended with intellectual generosity, sometimes blushed for Antony's antics and sometimes excoriated him. When Plutarch came to paint Antony's early character, he drew on the violent antipathy voiced by Cicero and other narrow critics, but there was enough in the portrait to make Antony recognizable:

All men of principle loathed his ill-timed drunkenness, his wasteful spending, his debauchery with women, his days spent in sleep or staggering about with a splitting headache, his nights of revelry watching fools and jesters or botched representations in vulgar mime. We are told that when he was feasting at the marriage of the mime Hippias he drank all night, and in the morning, as the people called him to the Forum, he came before them still stuffed with food and vomited into his toga, which a friend held at his service. Cytheris, a notorious actress from the same school of mime, was his great favourite, whom he carried about in a litter on his Italian travels, with as many attendants after her as followed his mother. People were scandalized at the sight of golden goblets waved about on pleasure-trips as if in a sacred procession, at the pitching of rich pavilions and the laying-out of costly feasts by meadows and groves, at his chariots drawn by lions, and at the commandeering of respectable houses to put up harlots and music-makers.

But the events of the civil war, the murder of his great

chief, the intrigues of the triumvirate, and the victory at Philippi appeared to make a more sober Antony. Back in Rome at the end of 42 BC, he shunned the disreputable life, quietly preparing himself for government in the East and for Caesar's uncompleted task – the conquest of Parthia – laid upon Antony as a holy duty. He was busy putting on the garments of responsibility, becoming the student of the hellenistic East, getting ready to be the keeper of client-kings and the pacifier of their ancient states. In all things he was the servant of Rome. But the wild man in him was only dormant, waiting to be tickled or prodded into recklessness. Adventures and temptations in eastern lands had unsettled steadier Romans than Antony.

At the beginning of 41 BC, when Antony arrived in Ephesus to take on the role in the East assigned to him by the triumvirs, the unflattering eye of Plutarch saw the old shambling beast starting to peep out beneath the proconsular dignity:

> When Antony made his entry into Ephesus, women dressed as Bacchantes and men and boys as Satyrs and Pans frisked in the procession before him. The city was draped with wreaths of ivy and thyrsus wands, the air sounded with brazen music of many instruments, and the people hailed him as the New Dionysus, the Benefactor and Bringer of Joy. This was how some people saw him, but to others he came as Dionysus the Cruel, the Eater of Flesh, for he ruined many noble families and gave their property to rogues and sycophants.

His task, which was to establish order after war and to raise money for more wars, was difficult and he went at it with a kind of misdirected enthusiasm, flinging benefits here and exacting cruel tributes there.

His character [Plutarch continued] was essentially simple and he was slow to see the truth. When he knew he was at fault, he was full of repentance and ready to satisfy those he had wronged. If he had to punish an offence or put right an injustice, he acted on the grand scale, and in the general view he overstepped the bounds far more in rewards than in punishments.

To some cities and princes he gave freedom, remission of taxes, new territory, even whole islands. Other poor citizens were screwed down to the last penny, ordered to pay nine years' taxes in the space of two years, which was at least more generous than the initial demand of ten years of taxes to be paid at once. For some he had special favours. Archelaus, a Cappadocian prince, was most fortunate because (or so it was rumoured) his mother Glaphyra was a beautiful woman and had taken Antony to her bed.

As he began to set up his administration Antony summoned all governors, princes and client-kings to his court to account for their actions and to be told of his plans. Egypt, richest and most powerful of the eastern kingdoms, figured boldly in these plans. Thirteen years before, as an officer with the army of Gabinius, he had seen the land at close quarters; he knew the potentiality of the country, and also the history and reputation of the queen. He wrote letters to Cleopatra summoning her to attend on him. He wanted her to explain Egypt's rather limp support for the triumvirs in the recent war with Cassius. She considered that her small foray with the fleet had shown enough enthusiasm, and otherwise she meant to keep to her usual policy of polite non-co-operation, saying perhaps and meaning no, while she tried to read the new pattern of the pieces in Rome. Antony persisted. He sent his loose, shifty, talented friend Quintus Dellius with a dangerous charm and some persuasive arguments. No doubt there was also a hint of threat. After a stately delay due to a goddess-queen of the most distinguished lineage in the Mediterranean world, during which Cleopatra had glimpsed a way to handle this importunate Roman, the queen set out to meet Antony at Tarsus in Asia Minor.

6

ANTONY
AND CLEOPATRA

THE SCENE, made ever-famous by Shakespeare, is best
given in the words of Plutarch, from whom Shakespeare
took his story:

She sailed up the River Cydnus in a barge with a poop of gold
and with purple sails, her rowers stroking the water with oars
of silver that kept time to the music of flutes and pipes and
lutes. As for Cleopatra herself, she reclined under a canopy of
cloth-of-gold, dressed as that Aphrodite we see in paintings,
while on either side stood pretty little Cupids who cooled her
with their fans. In her crew were the most beautiful of her
women clothed as Nereids and Graces, some at the helm,
others tending the tackle and the ropes of the barge, out of
which came a wondrous sweet smell of perfumes that wafted
over the river-banks. A multitude of people raced the river-
side to view her progress and the city emptied to see her. As
the crowds fled away, Antony sat enthroned in the marketplace to await the queen. At last, he was left sitting alone,

while the word spread on all sides that Aphrodite had come to play with Dionysus for the happiness of Asia.

Antony was the victor of Philippi, Caesar's general entering his appointed lands. Vain-glorious, bold and ruggedly hand-some, he was composed for pleasure, and he looked on the East as a harem of does awaiting its stag, though unfortunately this lordly Roman beast was married to Fulvia, a dominating Roman shrew. Cleopatra was twenty-eight, every inch an Egyptian queen, and in her prime, knowing, practised, clever.

> So she provided herself with a world of gifts [Plutarch wrote], stores of silver and gold, riches and sumptuous ornaments, all that her exalted position and the vast wealth of her realm could give her. But she had brought nothing in which she trusted more than in herself, and in the charm and grace and enchantment of her presence.

Whatever weapons she relied on, they were stronger than his: she, a guileful queen long experienced in the dark arts of politics, a woman with the sensuality to attract the best of heroes, and the capacity to know it and use it; he, a successful soldier who gave way too easily to indulgence, a strong valiant body allied to a warm but careless heart. The brief contest of the sexes, in which he was so utterly vanquished, is again related by Plutarch:

> Antony invited Cleopatra to dine with him, but she thought it more fitting that he should come to her; so most courteously he accepted and went. He found the preparations made for him magnificent beyond words. But what astonished him most was the infinite number of lights and torches, so artfully

Silver coin depicting Antony, *c.* 39 BC, at the
time of his marriage to Octavia.

arranged in devices and patterns, some round and some
square, that their brilliance amazed the eye and took the
breath away. Next day, Antony feasted her intending to sur-
pass her in magnificence and elegance, but he was hopelessly
outdone in both so that he, with his equal good spirits, was
the first to pour scorn on his own meagre entertainment.
Then Cleopatra saw that he had a soldierly humour, broad
and coarse, and she began to pay him in his own coin, teasing
him thoroughly and without fear.

For the details of this passionate adventure between two
strong personalities, Plutarch is our only guide. He wrote long
after the events but he relied on memoirs and personal
accounts handed down in his family from Alexandria, and on
writings of the time that have not survived. He was sufficiently
Greek to keep always in mind the humanity of his characters,
and the tragedy of their affair which is implicit in their fall
from high estate. In this sense, what he gives us is romance.

A Roman historian with access to such intimacies would surely have given us a harder view, with a wider political interpretation, and a heavy dose of moralistic propaganda. But Plutarch had the sensibility of an older world than ours, even in his view of romance, and he knew that before it became tragedy their love-making began with high policy on her part and high foolishness on his.

> He allowed the queen to carry him off to Alexandria, where he indulged himself in a waste of childish sports, squandering on idle pleasures what Antiphon calls the most precious of all commodities, which is time. For they gathered around them a group of friends whom they called the Inimitable Livers, and they gave banquets each day for one another of extraordinary expense.

> The royal cooks would prepare eight wild boars for a company of a dozen people, not that so much would be eaten, but everything had to be cooked and served to perfection, which might be ruined by a moment's delay.

> For Antony might eat at once, or in a little while, or he might call for wine first, or of a sudden take up some business. 'So we never prepare just one supper,' said the cook, 'but many of them, for we never know the moment he will wish to eat.'

They feasted and flirted and made fun out of both night and day, and Cleopatra played Antony as skilfully as she handled his fishing-line on their seaside gambols, baiting the hook and tricking him into the catch:

> Plato speaks of four kinds of flattery, but Cleopatra knew a

thousand. Whether Antony was serious or lighthearted, she knew a way to please him, and kept him in her sight night and day. She played dice with him, and drank with him, and hunted with him, and stood watching while he performed his exercise at arms. At night, he would dress like a slave and roam the city, peering into poor men's windows, scolding and making fun, and she would go with him as a maid-servant, taking part in his mad antics, even as he mocked and brawled and sometimes took home blows. But the fact was that the Alexandrians liked this buffoonery and jollity, and they played their part in all these games. They liked Antony with his jibes and his jokes, and used to say that he showed the Romans his tragic mask but kept the comic one for them.

Alexandria suited Antony well. It was a city of some wickedness and much licence where a man could devote himself as seriously to entertainment as to science and philosophy. The moral background was significantly different to that of Rome; a man was not condemned for imaginative misconduct, and extravagant display, so long as it was artistic, counted as a part of virtue. Antony was of good birth but rustic upbringing, with a father who was an improvident gambler. He had spread his wild oats among actresses and mimes. He married first the daughter of a freedman and then Fulvia who, though humbly born, made brave men quake. 'A private citizen', Plutarch wrote of her, 'was beneath her notice. She wanted to rule magistrates and give orders to generals.' To escape from this Roman harridan into the arms of the queen of Egypt was a strange bliss for Antony. Yet like many loose-living men with a disposition for heroic action, Antony found something intimidating in strong women, even when they led him on to further excess. As Plutarch commented wryly:

Cleopatra was indebted to Fulvia for the lessons she had given Antony in obedience to women. He was thoroughly tamed when the queen took him over.

Even in the realm of love, she was the queen and he was the subject.

The verdict of Plutarch, which was also a general opinion of the time, was clear enough. Antony was bewitched by a power beyond his control.

Such was Antony's nature that the love of Cleopatra came as the final and crowning mischief of all that could befall him. It roused to the point of madness many passions formerly concealed, or at least dormant; if any spark of goodness or hope to redeem him were left in him, Cleopatra quenched it straight and made all things worse than before.

As for Cleopatra, what did she want beyond the spice of slumming in late-night dives, or in the satisfaction given by a vigorous Roman body? In Tarsus, she had already begun to make her demands. She called for executions: Arsinoe, the younger sister who had so treacherously failed her first in Alexandria during Caesar's war and then in Ephesus where she dared to let herself be called the queen of Egypt; Serapion, the governor of Cyprus who had defected with ships and supplies to Cassius; and a deluded young man at Aradus who claimed to be her first brother-husband Ptolemy XIII, long since drowned in the waters of the Nile. In her kingdom there was only one monarch and one voice. Any other who claimed to speak in the name of authority could expect the extreme penalty of her law. Her first and greatest interests were the security of her throne and the safety of her country.

Antony's sin, in the eyes of history, was not so much the revelry and love-making in Alexandria but (as Plutarch noted) the waste of precious time. In the winter of 41 BC and into the next year Antony and Cleopatra played their games, and who is to doubt that they enjoyed themselves enormously? It was a carnal interlude. A world of pleasure unfolded, and Cleopatra knew better than to press her lover too hard. After she had received some small benefits, she read the book of his character and filed him away for the future. Antony had his excitement, but he got no money for his Roman ventures from her treasury. Nor could he yet rely on her unconditional support against Octavian, if it came to a contest between the triumvirs, as seemed very likely when Antony's wife Fulvia and his brother Lucius revolted against Octavian in Italy.

Idling in Alexandria, Antony had no knowledge of his family's rash actions in Italy. Fulvia and Lucius were defeated and driven into exile, but neither Antony nor Octavian was ready for a prolonged test of wills. Fulvia, blundering as ever, had given a foretaste of the inevitable, but for the moment it was expedient to patch up an agreement, for both leaders had their troubles elsewhere. In the eastern empire, Herod, the ruler installed by Antony in recognition of past services to Rome, was at odds with his own people. On the border of Judaea, Syria was uneasy, beginning to face the threat of a fresh attack from Parthia. Asia Minor was also in a state of nerves, the client-kings waiting to see if they should jump from Rome to Parthia. Most of all Parthia itself called into question Roman resolution and authority. The defeat of Crassus at Carrhae so long ago was still unavenged, Caesar's campaign of reconquest seemed less important than drinking and fondling in Alexandria, and now a belligerent Parthia was on the move once more.

In the spring of 40 BC the urgency of all the state business that Antony had wilfully neglected dragged him back to Italy. He had intended to go to Syria to prepare for the Parthian invasion but suddenly events in Italy were more pressing. On his journey he briefly met Fulvia in Greece, and having heard the story of her trouble-making he abandoned her to die in Sicyon. Sextus Pompeius, youngest son of the great Pompey, from this Sicilian base had made himself the master of the seas – he called himself 'Son of Neptune' and put the sea-god on his Sicilian coins. He had become a piratical but influential third force between Antony and Octavian, and he was sounding out Antony for plots and sympathy.

The two powerful triumvirs (poor Lepidus by now hardly counted) were offended with each other, bickering amid mutual accusations of ill-faith. After Philippi, Octavian had struggled with the thankless task of attempting to settle the veteran legionaries with gifts of land. To assimilate them into the Italian countryside caused a chaos in land-holding and farming, leading to a loss of agricultural production and some hardship from hunger. Also, Sextus' fleet was restricting the import of grain from the traditional markets in Egypt and North Africa. Italy needed a period of rest, consolidation and stability, as Octavian knew very well. Civil war was a gangrene in the body politic.

In October 40 BC Antony and Octavian met in Brundisium and warily made a new agreement. Lepidus was confined to North Africa from where he was later removed to complete his undistinguished life as *pontifex maximus* in Rome, a ritual office of no practical significance. Then the Roman world was divided in two along the line of the Adriatic Dalmation coast. Octavian took the West and Antony the East, though both had the right to recruit in Italy. And in the Roman way, to try

Basalt head of Octavia, Octavian's sister
and Mark Antony's second wife.

to seal bargains that would not stick, a political marriage of convenience was arranged. Octavian's well-loved elder sister, Octavia, a lady of noble virtue and the sweetest nature, was given to the libertine Antony. Both were recently widowed. Octavia was already pregnant by her deceased husband. And in Alexandria there was another pregnancy; Cleopatra expected the birth of Antony's twins.

After this pact, it seemed as if Antony would be permanently lost to Alexandria and to Cleopatra, the only mementoes of his gaudy stay being some riotous memories and his twin children. Newly-married and newly-respectable, Antony began keeping state in Athens with Octavia, but more like a

Greek Dionysus than a Roman Mars. As 39 slipped into 38 BC he still had not begun the great vengeance against Parthia, even though the Parthians had twice invaded the client-kingdoms of the East, the first time most shamefully under the Roman renegade Labienus. Antony's subordinates Ventidius and Pollio had contained Parthia with some hard-fought victories, won largely because the Parthians had temporarily abandoned their light-cavalry tactic of hit and run.

Nor were things going well in Italy. The treaty of Brundisium had settled nothing. Octavian and Antony were again in dispute about money and troops and spheres of influence. Sextus Pompeius still had a grip around Rome, strangling the gain-supply with his fleet. The term of office of the triumvirate was coming to an end and Antony needed to extend it. Encouraged by Octavia, who was torn between brother and husband, Antony went to Tarentum early in 37 BC in an angry mood, determined to out-face Octavian. For a moment the empire hung on the edge of war, which was averted in large part by Octavia's anguished diplomacy, and another treaty was arranged. But it was only a truce. Antony was convinced that Octavian was playing him false, and this was to some extent true (if truth could be found in the welter of recriminations), though Octavian's political determination and ceaseless hard work contrasted sharply with Antony's sloth in Athens. Antony was hardly satisfied. He did not trust Octavian, with good reason, and perhaps he no longer trusted Octavia. In Athens, she had borne him two children and was pregnant with a third. But half her heart was still with her brother. She was a good woman, no doubt, but was she sufficiently devoted to her husband? And virtue is often dull. Antony had had enough of Roman obduracy and Roman sobriety. He left Octavia and his children in Italy and went east again.

Antony turned his back on the West and on all the connections that had tied him to it. In those parts, Octavian might do as he pleased. The East was now wholly Antony's domain and he would play whatever tunes he wished on this vast tympanum. A thunder of war awaited him in Parthia but first, to soothe his bruised spirit, his mind turned to a little night-music. He threw away 'all those nobler considerations of restraint that might have saved him', Plutarch wrote. He sent one of his followers to bring Cleopatra to him in Syria.

The summons appeared to be no surprise to Cleopatra. She had kept her usual close intelligence on Roman affairs and saw how it now stood between Octavian and Antony. It was said that she had placed an Egyptian astrologer in Antony's court, and knew day by day the inclination of his mind. She arrived at Antioch with the twins whom their father had never seen – a powerful argument with a warm-hearted man – and a prepared course of action. She was looking for gifts, but not the jewels or ornaments that would settle a lover's estrangement.

> When she arrived [Plutarch continued] the presents he showered on her were no trifles. To the lands she already possessed he added Phoenicia, Coele Syria, the isle of Cyprus and a great part of Cilicia. He also gave her that portion of Judaea which produces balsam, and the Nabataean coast of Arabia down to the Red Sea.

Cleopatra's preoccupation was, as always, the strength of her kingdom and the security of her borders, especially the dangerous frontier in the east of Egypt that let on to a huge tract of dust and mountain where dynasts with puzzling histories fought to save themselves from the Roman onrush.

That frontier at Pelusium was the weak point of Egypt, trampled time and again by invasion, and the policy to guard the vulnerable point by taking firm footholds in Palestine and Syria and along the Arabian coast had been set out and successfully implemented long ago by her great predecessor Ptolemy II Philadelphus. In wanting the lands given to her by Antony, Cleopatra was only drawing on the wisdom of her royal house. Behind the soft moments of her dalliance with Antony lay the resolution of an iron will and a cool understanding of statecraft. What did it matter to her that Lysanias must be executed so that his kingdom of Chalcis might add to the greater safety of Egypt? Antony gave way, and Cleopatra gave her tigress' purr. Then between caresses she pushed a little further for the kingdom of Herod. But Judaea and Herod were too important to Antony and he would not budge. Cleopatra gained only the balsam groves and Herod's undying enmity.

Naturally, Antony's generosity did not please Rome.

In the past [wrote Plutarch] Antony had given territories and principalities to private men, and he had deprived many rulers of their kingdoms. But none of this caused as much offence to Romans as the extraordinary gifts he granted Cleopatra. And he made matters worse when he acknowledged his twin children by her, whom he named Alexander and Cleopatra, and surnamed Sun and Moon. Antony, however, was well-versed in the art of cloaking shameful deeds with fine words, and he declared that the greatness of the Roman empire was in the bestowing of kingdoms, not in taking them, and that nobility was increased by a succession born of many sovereigns.

Egyptian chalkstone relief showing Cleopatra as Isis. She is depicted wearing
the head-dress of the Mother-goddess Mut, surmounted by the horns
of the Cow-goddess Hathor and the disk of the Moon.

ABOVE: The main temple at Denderah is dedicated to Hathor, goddess of love and beauty. It dates mainly from the Ptolemaic period but probably occupies the site of a much older temple.

BELOW: The Sacred Lake or Cleopatra's Pool at Denderah.

The sandstone relief on the outside south wall of the temple of Hathor
at Denderah shows Cleopatra with Caesarion, her son by Julius Caesar,
as Isis and Horus offering to the gods. Caesarion is depicted
as a pharaoh offering incense.

ABOVE: Marble bust of Mark Antony.

BELOW: This Pompeiian wall painting shows Roman galleys engaged in a sea battle.

Detail of a marble statue of Octavian who assumed the title of Emperor
Augustus Caesar a few years after he had won the Battle of Actium in 31 BC.
1st century AD copy of an original dating from *c.* 20 BC.

The deaths of Antony and Cleopatra have been wildly romanticized over the years by various artists.

RIGHT: Illumination from a medieval manuscript depicting the tomb of Mark Antony and Cleopatra.

BELOW: *The Death of Antony and Cleopatra* by Alessandro Turchi (1579–1649).

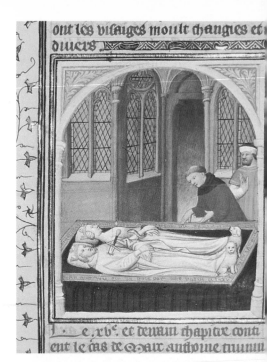

The Death of Cleopatra by Jean-Baptiste Regnault (1754–1829)

After the annexation of Egypt by Octavian in 30 BC Egyptian themes became
even more popular in Roman decorative arts. This second-century AD
mosaic from Tivoli shows a boat trip on the river Nile.

Antony added that his paragon Heracles had scattered his seed widely, not relying on the posterity of a single womb.

He never feared the audit of his copulations, but let Nature have her way, and become the foundation of many families.

Did Antony and Cleopatra now enter into a form of marriage? It is likely, though the historical evidence is not certain. But in any case their destinies were beginning to run together. Roman law permitted Antony only one wife, and she was Octavia. But by his many actions Antony had repudiated that law and morality. The looser habits of the orient suited him better. And the marriage customs of the Ptolemies were lax indeed. At a later date Antony certainly considered himself married to Cleopatra, and at this time the two lovers began to put the image of their heads on each other's coins. Cleopatra was sure at last that she had found the Roman most likely to save Egypt from Rome, and she intended to bring him to her, not just with the wiles of sex and pleasure, but with children and marriage and the symbolism of kingship. If he was Dionysus, as he claimed to be in all lands to the east of Athens, then once again she was Isis, the goddess-queen. Their lives were intertwined, in ambition, in bed, and in joint deification according to the ancient custom of the East.

All this was a matter of hard policy for Cleopatra, whatever the pleasures of their meeting, but to Antony it was an imaginative stroke in a dream-like plan. Already Dionysus, he was now thinking of himself as a second Alexander. The conquests that Antony hoped to make in Parthia, following steps already imprinted by Alexander, would give him a fame to rival that of the Macedonian conqueror. And a conjunction with Cleopatra would lend legitimacy to his claim, for the Ptolemies were the

successors of Alexander, the last and most successful of his followers. It was no idle whim that made Antony name his twins
Alexander Helios and Cleopatra Selene. The rise of a young
Sun and a young Moon gave promise of a new Golden Age
and rang out a challenge to the Parthians, whose king styled
himself 'brother of the Sun and Moon'. The symbolism illu-
minated this un-Roman dream in which a new Alexander
joined to a long-ruling Ptolemy would march to eastern glory.
Cleopatra, in her shrewd way, pitched her dream at a lower
level. It was enough for her that she should make her dynasty
safe, guided by ancestral light. In 36 BC, when she gave birth
to Antony's third child, she named the baby Ptolemy Philadelphus in honour of the king who had achieved so much for
Egypt.

But it was a fault with Antony that he dreamed too much
and acted too little. It was time to go to work. Though the
Parthian campaign had been put off for many years, in the
winter of 37–6 BC Antony started to make strenuous preparations. A new king, Phraates IV, reigned in Parthia, a prince
who had killed his father Orodes because the old man was too
long in dying. As Antony had been idle before, now he was all
energy. He gathered his Roman legions, many of them composed of veterans from Spain and Gaul, and summoned the
client-kings to send their armed contingents. A large army
collected in Armenia, perhaps as many as 100,000, a force that
made 'the Indians beyond Bactria and all Asia tremble'.
Cleopatra went with Antony and the army as far as the
Euphrates and then turned back for Egypt, intending to visit
on the way the new territories granted her so recently. In particular, she wanted to go through Judaea, to make sure that
her old enemy Herod would not stand in the way of the
income due to her from the balsam groves.

The hostile account that the historian Josephus wrote of this journey showed just how much Cleopatra disturbed the delicate equilibrium of the East, and how much men feared her influence with an Antony they judged to be besotted beyond reason:

King Herod turned all his personal treasures into cash and sent it to Antony. Even so, he could not buy freedom from all trouble; for Antony, ruined by his passion for Cleopatra, had become the complete slave of his desire, while Cleopatra struck right through her own family till not a single relative was left alive. And thirsting now for the blood of strangers, she was slandering the princes of Syria and urging Antony to have them executed, hoping in this way to become mistress of all their possessions. She even extended her greed to Jews and Arabs, working in secret to get their kings Herod and Malchus put to death.

Antony was sober enough to realize that one part of her demands – the killing of honest men and famous kings – was utterly immoral. But he cut them to the heart by withdrawing his friendship. He lopped a large part off their territories, including the palm-grove at Jericho in which the balsam is produced, and gave it to Cleopatra together with all the cities south of the river Eleutherus except Tyre and Sidon. Mistress now of this domain she escorted Antony as far as the Euphrates on his way to fight the Parthians, and then came by way of Apamea and Damascus into Judaea. Herod placated her with costly gifts, and leased back from her the lands broken from his kingdom, at 200 talents a year!

This was Cleopatra, the queen of sharp practice, the astute woman of business who husbanded the resources of Egypt so carefully, and even found time to run her own woollen-mill in Alexandria staffed by her waiting-women.

When Cleopatra left him in May 36 BC, Antony went north from Zeugma with the arrogant confidence of a Roman general at the head of the invincible legions. He was an intrepid commander of men and a fine cavalry tactician, but he was not a good strategist and the conduct of a difficult campaign eluded him. The usual road into Parthia lay along a more southerly route, but Antony intended to make a bold swing to the north and the east to approach the Parthian capital, Ecbatana, from an unexpected direction. At first, the march went well. But by the time the army reached Phraaspa, in the land of the Medes, the campaign began to stall though oversight, folly and some bad luck. Antony failed to secure his rear in Armenia, where the king was only loosely bound to him by fear not love. The Roman wagon-train was too slow and too vulnerable, which forced Antony to divide his army to guard it. And the enemy, who had good intelligence of his plans, had started to use again their devastating light-cavalry tactics, never challenging the full force of the Roman onslaught but firing and then vanishing under the perpetual cloud of their arrows. Antony was forced to turn back. The retreat of 27 days through mountains unknown to the army to the base-camp in Armenia was a chapter of horrors, menaced all the way by the deadly buzz of the Parthian arrows, toiling amid extremes of privation from hunger, fatigue and exposure. Though at one point Antony thought of suicide, in the worse circumstances he showed his best qualities, his strength and endurance, his comradely spirit, his open-hearted generosity under adversity and his care for his poor suffering troops.

Many reasons inspired the devotion of his men [wrote

Plutarch who was never an uncritical admirer of Antony]
namely his nobility, his eloquence, his simplicity, his extravagant generosity, the familiar and genial manner of his daily
conduct. His heart was with his men, and he shared their distress, and tended to them in their woe, so that even the
wounded and the sick were ready to serve him – as ready or
even more so as the strong and the healthy.

But having given this affecting tribute to Antony's great
qualities, Plutarch must then return to the familiar criticism
and place the real blame for the failure of the campaign on the
witch of Egypt.

Such was his passion to spend the winter with her that he
took the field too early in the season and conducted a campaign without good order. It was as if he were no longer the
master of his own judgement, but rather under some magic
spell; for his eyes seemed to be constantly going back to her
image. His thoughts were fixed upon his return rather than
on defeating the enemy.

Antony's military errors were his own, not Cleopatra's. But
the accusations against her of magic, or of a drug-induced
influence, began to become the common-place of history.

If not wounded, then sinking from dropsy and dysentery,
the soldiers of the legions limped back to Armenia. Here,
however, Antony could no longer rely on the goodwill of the
king and the inhabitants, so he pulled further back, with
another increase in hardship, to the Syrian coast near Sidon.
In this miserable campaign he lost some 30,000 men. Hurt in
body and reputation, Antony like a chastized schoolboy
wanted comfort. He also needed money and supplies, which

Cleopatra could give him. He sent for her but she was slow in coming and the black mood descended on him, for he lacked the resolution patiently to endure this uncertainty.

> He became distraught and took to heavy drinking. He could not endure the waiting but would jump up from the table to look for her arrival. At last, she came by sea with large quantities of clothing and money, though some accounts say that she came with clothing only, and that Antony took money from his own private funds to distribute to the soldiers as if it were a gift from her.

This last statement sounded like Roman propaganda; but it would not have been out of character for Cleopatra. She was always very careful with the resources of the state, and would not have been keen to squander the contents of her treasury on an unlucky Roman venture in the wilds of Parthia. It was not in her plans to pay to avenge Roman defeat or to salve Roman pride.

For Antony, the Parthian campaign could only be unfinished business that left him with a tarnished reputation. He was anxious to pursue the war, but many of his best veterans were dead, and a large part of his army was destroyed. He needed money, but more immediately he needed fresh troops, which Octavian in Italy was not disposed to send him. After eight years of prudence, steadfast effort, canny political scheming and manipulation, Octavian's position was secure, even triumphant, in the West. With the advice of Maecanas and the military support of Agrippa, the most brilliant naval commander of the day, Octavian had defeated Sextus Pompeius whom Antony, very honourably, had refused to support. Octavian had eased Lepidus out of North Africa, released the flow of grain into Italy, finally settled his legionaries in a newly-pacified country, and so created the conditions for peaceful economic prosperity.

> I cleared the seas of pirates [Octavian wrote in his fragment of autobiography] and in that war I captured 30,000 fugitive slaves, who had taken up arms against the state, and I returned them to their masters.

And his good opinion of himself was shared by the senate and the people. 'After prolonged unrest', said the inscription put up for him in the Forum by the senate, 'he restored peace by land and sea.' Not without good reason was Octavian now hailed as Caesar Divi Filius. Only Antony in the East stood between him and the unpartitioned Roman world. On his own silver coins Octavian placed the figure of Apollo, god of light and order; on Antony's coins was Dionysus, the dark god of mystery and violence.

For most observers, the reasons for a final conflict were now in view. Mists of uncertainty had been burnt away by success in the West and failure in the East, and the contestants stood starkly differentiated. All this was easily seen. Only Antony befuddled by misplaced dreams and frustration was not yet sure. Cleopatra knew it and at last was ready to throw down her gambler's hand on the side of Antony. Things had gone so far she could not avoid his fate, for good or bad. Octavian, most clear-sighted of all, knew it, but for the sake of the sister he loved so well he would not yet move against Antony. For Octavia, with the serene confidence of a good woman, refused to abandon her husband, though she knew to the last scandal the follies he committed with Cleopatra. Antony was her husband and there was no more to be said.

She would defend and support him to the grave.

There never was a chance that Octavia, for all her tender virtue, would prevail on her husband. To a man under the influence of the Egyptian queen, goodness and constancy were poor companions. In March 35 BC, as soon as she could organize shipping and supplies, Octavia set out for the East with aid for Antony, as Cleopatra had done some months before. She had with her such troops and stores as her brother Octavian was willing to provide, but these were less than were owed to Antony under the terms of the treaty of Tarentum. She never got to deliver them. At Athens she received a peremptory message from Antony ordering her to send on the ships but to return to Rome herself, and as an obedient wife she went. She returned to the house in Rome to look after not only her own daughters by Antony, but also his sons by Fulvia; she became a figure in the city whose every dignified step admonished Antony and sent a dart of anger into Octavian's heart.

In 35 BC Antony was spared any further challenges from Parthia by the internal rivalries of that kingdom. But he remembered that the Armenians had abandoned him and needed to be taught a lesson. In January 34 BC he invaded Armenia with his rested and reinforced legions. He subdued the country and captured King Artavasdes and two of his sons, though the rumour put about by Octavian's adept writers suggested that these captives had been taken by treachery, not in battle. By the autumn of 34 BC, flush with this success, Antony was back in Alexandria with Cleopatra.

In the scale of conquests, the success in Armenia was nothing very much. But it needed recognition, if only for the sake of Antony's self-esteem, and Cleopatra was ready to indulge him. Alexandria, a city well-used to grand spectacle, was granted the extraordinary sight of a Roman triumph a world away from the Capitol in Rome. Romans, who were always jealous of their ancient practices and privileges, found in this show a subtle insult to the traditions of their people. But Cleopatra, looking back as ever to the former greatness of the Ptolemies and drawing her inspiration from their royal deeds, perhaps had in mind the celebratory processions of Ptolemy II Philadelphus, for the event in Antony's honour was given an Alexandrian gloss. Cleopatra sat on a golden throne, awaiting the arrival of Antony's triumphal chariot, leading through the city the Armenian captives and the spoils of war. This was not so much an exultation of a Roman general. It was a representation of Egyptian Isis welcoming to her court the god Dionysus after his dangerous wanderings in the East. It was a homecoming as much as a celebration of victory, and the un-Roman nature of the occasion was made clear by Antony's clemency when he spared the life of the treacherous King Artavasdes. Julius Caesar had spared the life of Arsinoe, but she was only a young girl. Cold-blooded Octavian, truly Roman in his calculated cruelty as in all else, would never have allowed such cloudy generosity to come between him and sound policy.

This Alexandrian diversion – this almost-Roman triumph – was followed by another that was even more strange, which startled as much as it gave offence, as Plutarch reported:

Antony assembled a great number of people in the gymnasium, and there on a high dais of silver he set two golden thrones, one for himself and the other for Cleopatra, with smaller thrones for his children. Then he openly proclaimed Cleopatra as Queen of Egypt, Cyprus, Libya and Coele Syria, and named Caesarion as her consort. This youth was reputed to be the son of Julius Caesar, who had left

Cleopatra pregnant. Next, he proclaimed his own sons by Cleopatra to be Kings of Kings. To Alexander he gave Armenia, Media and Parthia (as soon as it might be conquered), and to Ptolemy he gave Phoenicia, Syria and Cilicia. And then he presented his sons to the people, Alexander in the dress of the Medes, with long gown and high, narrow hat, and Ptolemy clothed in the old Macedonian way with boots and short cloak and broad hat circled by a royal diadem, for such was the old attire of the successors to Alexander the Great. When the children had saluted and kissed their parents they went their way, one with an Armenian guard of honour, the other with a Macedonian. As for Cleopatra, at this time and on all other public occasions she wore the robes of the goddess Isis, and came before her subjects as the New Isis.

So that the message should not be lost or misconstrued Antony had a coin struck. On one side was his own head with the inscription *Armenia conquered*; on the other side was Cleopatra's head and the legend *Queen of Kings and of her Sons who are Kings*.

These Donations of Alexandria were in name the gift of Antony, but Cleopatra had the greater glory, and who can doubt that she was the mastermind behind the whole portentous demonstration? Antony's own position was left carefully undefined. In the East he was the New Dionysus. But to his legions he was plain Marcus Antonius, Roman citizen and general, and they followed him in this capacity. He could do nothing that would alienate their loyalty, which fundamentally belonged to Rome. Whatever brilliant plumage he might wear in the Alexandrian court, Antony must appear before his soldiers in unaffected Roman guise or else his authority in the empire would be nothing.

Cleopatra was not constrained by such scruples. Without striking a single war-like blow she had secured for her Ptolemaic dynasty an inheritance that included by far the greater part of the eastern Roman empire. And she was beginning to permit herself a new dream. Already, her consort Ptolemy Caesar – Caesarion – gave some colour to a claim, weak though it was, for recognition from Rome. Now the documents of her realm were beginning to appear with a double dating that had nothing to do with her official co-ruler Ptolemy Caesar. This dating stemmed from 37 BC, the year of her conjunction – her formal marriage? – with Antony in Antioch, and recognized not only the years of her own reign but also the regnal years of Antony. With the greatest daring she had incorporated the Roman ruler of the East – the de facto Imperator of the Eastern Empire – into her royal family. Cleopatra was the Egyptian goddess-queen. Now it seemed that she was also on her way to becoming the empress of Rome. She began to use as her customary oath a formula that said 'as surely as I shall one day give judgement in the Capitol'.

In amazement and some apprehension Romans began to wonder how all this had happened. With a good knowledge of Antony's faults they preferred to credit her triumphs, not to intelligence or clear policy, but to sexual manipulation. Plutarch, whose later history voiced much of this Roman prejudice, had many stories of the tricks she played for Antony's love:

> She pretended to be consumed with the most passionate love
> for Antony, taking little food so that she seemed to be pining
> away. When Antony was near she would fix on him a look of
> rapture, and when he left she would languish and seem on the

verge of collapse. She was often seen in tears, which she would hurriedly wipe away, as if to hide them.

Her creatures and flatterers also worked hard on Antony. They told him that he must be a callous brute with a heart of stone, since here was a mistress utterly devoted to him alone, and his coldness was killing her. His marriage to Octavia, so they said, was only a political convenience for her brother's sake. Octavia enjoyed the title of wife, but Cleopatra, who was queen of many nations, had been content to be called his mistress, nor did she shun this name or think it unworthy of her so long as she could see him and be with him all her life. If he drove her away it would be the death of her. In the end they so melted and unmanned him that he truly began to believe that she would die if he left her.

Whatever the truth of these stories, certainly Cleopatra knew the uses of sexuality. She also had the theatricality of the Ptolemies, those practised deceivers, and could act with the best of them. Her dress and looks and conduct were well-calculated. A little book on the use of cosmetics appeared under her name, and though she may not have written it, at least it showed that in the common mind she knew those arts. She dressed carefully for effect, usually in the Greek costume of Alexandria, but when the occasion demanded it in the full majesty of the Egyptian Isis. To her, her whole persona was an artifice of state, to impress her subjects, to lend dignity to her monarchy, and to let her play, if need be, on the susceptible male heart.

Later Roman writers, in the grip of the virulent Roman propaganda that Octavian had encouraged against her, went from criticism to coarse abuse. Lucan, untrustworthy and foul-minded as ever, claimed that Pothinus the eunuch had said that men's lives were at risk, if they would not sleep with her: 'We are guilty in her eyes, like every other man who has not slept with her.' Propertius called her 'lecherous Canopus's harlot queen', who wore her servants out with sex and conducted a 'filthy' union with Antony.

> She became so debauched [Sextus Aurelius added] that she frequently offered herself as a common whore; but she was so beautiful that many men bought a night with her at the price of their own death.

The contemporary records of her reign, particularly from Alexandria where many hated her and found good reason to vilify and libel her, mention nothing of this sexual depravity. In a life of 39 years she had four children by two men. She conceived easily enough, but in an age without adequate contraception there is no record of further pregnancies, apart from Cicero's malicious rumour of a miscarriage, and even that baby would have been Julius Caesar's. At home, no sexual scandal touched her, even in the long periods between 41 and 32 BC when Antony was busy with his wars. In her imperious mind it is likely that she regarded herself as bound in a form of marriage first to Caesar and then, after his death, to Antony. These were not, and could never have been, marriages in the strict Roman form, but according to the fashion of the Ptolemies who in these matters made their own rules. And all the evidence shows that, far from being a wanton woman, she was constant to the two Romans in her life.

Nor, indeed, was sexual morality ever at the heart of the contention between Cleopatra and Rome. Great Romans were themselves notoriously loose in their affairs. Julius Caesar had been a rampant stallion, as his admiring troops loved to remind him. In his loves Antony was no worse than Octavian. The difference was that Antony appeared openly amorous, while Octavian clothed his bed-work with hypocrisy, as Antony sharply told him. Suetonius, the historian of the Caesars, quoted a letter of this time from Antony to Octavian:

> What's come over you? Is it because I go to bed with the queen? And what about you, is Livia the only woman you bed? I congratulate you if, at the time you read this letter, you haven't also had Tertullia or Terentilla or Rufilla or Salvia Titisenia or the whole lot of them. Does it really matter where you get your erection, or who the woman was?

Antony was genuinely indignant. He said firmly that Cleopatra was his wife, and if she was Egyptian, so what? Had not Octavian been willing to offer his daughter Julia to a Dacian prince?

The truth was that Rome had now begun to fear Cleopatra, and the accusation of depravity was only a convenient stick with which to beat her. She was portrayed as a witch of the orient, a voracious fertility goddess of an alien culture who unmanned Roman probity, and the hunting-dogs of the writer's yellow trade were set on her, in support, as always, of the ascendant power. But a greater mystery than her supposed sexual appetite was the extent and brilliance of her aura which engulfed the Roman intentions of Antony, and eventually lost him in the Alexandrian quagmire where he forgot both his military duty and Octavia. This was a triumph of personality that Rome could not understand.

Octavian, for one, did not want to try to understand, nor was it necessary from the point of view of his policy for him to do so. From his distance he saw an unstable Rome general, derelict in sense and duty, and now becoming a danger to all Rome's interests, not only in the East, but through Cleopatra's vanity for imperial power even in the Italian heartland. He saw also a studied insult to his sister Octavia, which was also an offence to himself. Antony had hatched a dream in Cleopatra's bed, a vision of a Hellenistic-Roman monarchy taking its forms from Ptolemaic tradition and relying on the ancient productive mass of Egypt for its prosperity. Sober Octavian was not led astray by impossible dreams. He worked steadily according to the usual Roman method of expansion by cautious conquests and by the patronage of client-kingdoms, but all firmly and solely under the authority of Rome. Nothing could reconcile the opposing visions of Antony and Octavian.

The coldness between them began with mutual accusations of bad faith and neglected promises, and progressed, particularly on the part of Octavian, to sneers about lack of probity, sobriety and competence. He brought up Antony's sexual misdemeanours and also his military failures in the East. Antony retaliated with contemptuous memories of Octavian's less than glorious conduct at the battle of Philippi (where Antony's generalship had been decisive), and of his feeble lack of spirit against Sextus Pompeius. 'He could not bear to look straight at the battle,' said Antony, 'but lay on his back stupidly staring at the sky and did not stir until the hostile fleet had been routed by Agrippa.' And as for sexual games, Antony hinted that Octavian had won Caesar's favour by homosexual pandering.

By pre-arrangement, the two consuls in Rome for the year 32 BC were both supporters of Antony. But they did not dare to reveal to the senate the Donations of Alexandria which Antony had made in favour of his own children. Instead, the consul Sosius delivered a strong indictment of Octavian which he answered in person but surrounded by an armed posse of friends and soldiers. The senate broke up and the two factions divided irrevocably. The consuls and some 400 senators fled to Antony in Asia Minor, leaving Rome completely in the hands of Octavian.

The arrival of his senatorial supporters in Ephesus steadied Antony's nerve. Accompanied by Cleopatra, he was once again all energy, an experienced general preparing for his last campaign. He had by his side his co-ruler and co-deity, and the queen of Egypt was now fully committed to him in war as in peace. At last, she opened her Egyptian treasury for his benefit and provided him with a sum that might have amounted to the huge figure of 20,000 talents, roughly the whole Egyptian income for one year. She also gave him a part of the Egyptian fleet and about 150 supply ships. Antony now had the resources to gather his army and he sent out the usual summonses to the client-kings. They came with their oaths of allegiance and their soldiers and were accepted, all but Herod whose presence Cleopatra could never stomach. He was sent away to gather the tribute owed to Cleopatra from her balsam groves in Judaea, but before he departed the Jewish fox (so Josephus tells us) confided to Antony that his best chance of success was to murder Cleopatra and seize Egypt as quickly as possible.

Octavian was dismayed by the speed and purpose of the preparations being made in Asia Minor.

> For he himself [Plutarch wrote] was not only very short of supplies but also immediately made himself unpopular by the taxes he had to impose. Citizens were made to pay a quarter of their income and freedmen one eighth of their property, which fell heavy on both, and caused a violent outcry and many disturbances all over Italy. For this reason, it was a great

error that Antony did not make war at once, since the delay allowed Octavian time to prepare. Also, in this period of inaction the indignation subsided; for people were angry when the money was taken from them, but once they had paid their temper cooled.

Antony had followed the custom of great men and lodged his will with the Vestal Virgins in Rome, where it was supposed to be sacrosanct until he died. But Octavian wrung the will from their grasp and read to the senate those passages likely to offend Romans. Particularly obnoxious to the senators was the clause that Antony's body, even if he died in Rome, should be taken back to Cleopatra in Egypt. Other charges were raised against the frivolity, luxury and weak irresponsibility of the lovers:

He had given her the library of Pergamon containing 200,000 scrolls; at a banquet before a large company he had risen from his place, and at the whim of some wager or jest had anointed her feet; he had permitted the Ephesians to salute her as their own queen, even in his presence; and on many occasions, seated in a tribunal to give justice to kings and tetrarchs, he had received love letters from her on tablets of onyx or crystal, and he had read them through in the full face of the public.

By implication, this was clearly degenerate conduct by a man drunk with lust for the Egyptian sorceress, a Roman no longer worthy of the name.

But still Antony delayed. Was it the difficulty of putting together the expedition, or the caresses of Cleopatra that held him back? In April 32 BC they moved to the island of Samos, a step closer to Italy. Octavian was collecting his fleet at Tarentum and Brundisium across the Adriatic. He was also strengthening his hold on Italy, recently shaken by the outcry against his taxes. Each town in Italy swore a *conjuratio*, a solemn oath of allegiance to Octavian, and this oath was repeated in the provinces of the West as far apart as North Africa and Gaul.

In May, Antony removed the base of his operations to Athens, a place of poignant and impressive memories for both him and Cleopatra. For it was in this most famous of ancient western cities that Cleopatra found the roots of her Ptolemaic Greek culture; and it was here that Antony and Octavia had spent the brief interval of their married days together, where both had been much reverenced by the Athenians.

The propaganda of insult between the opponents continued, drawing from Antony an outraged reply when he was accused of being a drunken sot. He was so riled that he answered with a little pamphlet from his own hand entitled *De ebrietate sua* ('On his Drunkenness'). To help them forget this and other unpleasantness, a statue of Cleopatra as Isis was placed on the Acropolis, next to the figure of Antony as Dionysus. But the memory of Octavia still lingered in Athens, and Cleopatra wished to rid herself of this ghost from the past. She prevailed on Antony to send Octavia a bill of divorcement, forcing her to quit Antony's house in Rome with her little flock of children, both his and hers, clinging about her.

Into the winter of 32 BC the rumour in Rome still played on the debauchery of the lovers frittering time away in Athens. It was said that Cleopatra poisoned the atmosphere of Antony's court, making men jumpy and discontented and ready to run away.

Coin depicting both Antony and Cleopatra,
issued in Asia Minor 32–31 BC.

Her parasites [wrote Plutarch] drove away many friends of
Antony, who found the drunken antics and foolishness of
these creatures more than they could stand. Many left at this
time including Dellius the historian, who was told by Glaucus
the physician that Cleopatra was plotting against his life. It
seems that he had offended her at dinner when he complained at the sour wine, while [he said] even Octavian's
favourite page, a pretty boy, was drinking Falernian in Rome.

Weather, not debauchery, was delaying the expedition.
Antony had missed the last sailing season, and naval operations did not begin in the winter. Antony's force was marking
time in Athens, according to normal military practice, but
Octavian was eager to suggest more sinister explanations:

Octavian also made it known that Antony was befuddled by
drugs, no longer master of his actions, and that Rome would
fight this war against the eunuch Mardian, against Pothinus,

Iras the queen's hairdresser, and Charmian her waiting-woman, for it was they who governed Antony's empire now.

Whatever the expected opposition, Octavian was taking no chances, making careful military preparations and giving legal form and substance to all his war-like actions. His plans were almost complete. One of his generals was sent to guard North Africa, roving naval squadrons kept watch along the coasts of Spain and Gaul. He put his chief counsellor Maecenas in charge of Rome and Italy. The main fleet, under the command of Agrippa and Octavian himself, waited in the ports of southern Italy for the passing of the winter storms.

In January 31 BC Octavian became consul for the third time, the highest republican office in Rome that he was due to share with Antony. But Octavian now had the government of the West so firmly in his hands that he was able to impose upon the senate to strike Antony out of the triumvirate and to bar him from the consulship. Then Octavian, as priest of the Roman people, went in solemn procession to the temple of Bellona, Goddess of War. Outside the temple, on the Field of Mars, he hurled a blood-tipped spear in the direction of the enemy and declared a *justum bellum* – a just war – against Cleopatra only. In this way he preserved the fiction that the coming struggle was not an episode in the long-running civil war. That great Roman unhappiness, according to the official propaganda, had been brought to an end through the statemanship of Octavian in 36 BC. This new war was a patriotic response to an invasion by an Egyptian queen.

Now the clash of arms could no longer be prevented. Both sides were committed beyond return. The new year came in with signs and portents, as if nature herself mirrored the agitation in the state. The message of the gods was written in the skies and etched into the earth, and it was a matter of desperate importance for mankind to read it right.

Pisaurum, a city colonized by Antony on the coast of the Adriatic, was shattered by earthquake. A statue of Antony in Alba did sweat continually, though wiped dry again and again. At Patras, the temple of Heracles was struck by lightning and burnt. In Athens, a statue of Dionysus was torn loose from its place in the War of the Giants and hurled by the storm into the theatre. Now, Antony claimed to be descended from Heracles, and since the manner of his life resembled that of Dionysus, men called him also the New Dionysus. This same storm, moreover, toppled the colossal statues in Athens of Eumenes and Attalus, those called 'the Antonians', while other figures nearby went undisturbed. And lastly, a dreadful sign appeared on Cleopatra's flagship, the Antonias. Swallows had nested under the stern, but others attacked them, drove them out, and killed their young.

If the gods had spoken, as the people of the age devoutly believed, then the portents were ominous for Antony.

7

ACTIUM
AND THE COURSE
OF HISTORY

O LD HISTORIES often assign large effects to slight
causes, seeing the fall of empires implicit in a single sin,
in human weakness, faults and wrong steps. Unlike the
ancients or Pascal, the seventeenth-century French philosopher, who found historical consequences in the length of
Cleopatra's nose, today we put our explanatory faith in the
interplay of economic forces, social aims, patterns of material
production, class structures, demographic change and the like.
But Pascal was not wholly wrong. Unforeseen events flow
from vagaries of character, and private whims may lead to the
death of thousands.

All the world knew that Cleopatra and Antony were vulnerable humans, but in what way were they guilty of charac-
teristic sins? The Roman philosopher Seneca judged Antony
to be a great man who 'was led astray into foreign ways and
un-Roman vices by his love of drink and his equal passion
for Cleopatra'. The poet Horace, friend of Maecenas and

supporter of Octavian but too sunny a temperament for vindictive abuse, thought that Cleopatra's mind had become 'clouded and disordered by Mareotic wine'. In the final pages of Plutarch, as the end approached for Antony and Cleopatra, there are many stories of gloomy carousing in a court vacillating between false hopes and despair. Antony had undermined his strong frame from a young age, turning night into day and reeling home at sun-up. He was now over fifty and his thickening waist was a measure of thickening wits. He was not without energy or capacity, but now they came intermittently in smaller loads dredged from a muddied well. He was on the last track to an uncertain destination, carried forward by the devils of his past. The taunt of tipsy revelry stung Antony, no doubt because it was largely true; it was the only accusation that he deigned to defend at length, in his *De ebrietate sua*.

With Cleopatra, there is no evidence of drunkenness. She also did the night rounds in Alexandria, but so far as one can see she drank cunningly, keeping Antony company, to entrap him in a web of indulgence. She wore on her finger a ring bearing a picture of Methe, goddess of drunkenness, but set in an amethyst, the stone of sobriety. This was a paradox of eastern mysticism, a celebration of the Sober Drunkenness propounded in her own Alexandria by the Jewish mystical philosopher Philo. This elated state was very far from the stupid excess of an alcoholic, rather it was a Dionysian initiation into a state of ecstatic joy that had the raised consciousness given by drink without its disgusting and enfeebling misery. In wearing the ring of Methe, Cleopatra was declaring her mastery over the goddess, not her subservience.

The second part of the charge in Seneca's indictment, that Antony had lost himself out of 'passion for Cleopatra', had much truth in it. Their affair, which had begun with calculated policy on her side and an insouciant desire for lust, luxury and possession on his, had developed into an entanglement of the whole person, so that neither quite knew where the domain of the one ended and the other began. They had come to need each other, beyond sex, beyond excitement, but desperately, and as in all desperate compulsions there was as much pain in it as pleasure. What had begun as a sordid adventure had grown into a heartfelt tragedy, for neither could go on without the other, and yet neither could succeed with the other. Their joint ambition, to be co-rulers of a Roman-Egyptian world, was impossible without each other, but could never be realized with each other.

Antony needed Cleopatra for very practical reasons. Almost alone in the East, she had the money and the resources to finance and supply his challenge to Octavian. And her efficient help for Antony showed her competence as queen of Egypt. Ship-building, provision of the fleet, storage and movement of very large amounts of grain, transport, payment for men and material, all fell to Cleopatra, and she managed these tasks despite the seasonal difficulties of Egyptian agriculture and the turmoil of the Roman wars just beyond her borders. When there was a shortage of timber for the new ships, the docks at Berytos in the Lebanon were placed under Egyptian administration, to organize the felling and supply of cedars from the interior. All this was done by her authority, her single voice in command of the centralized Ptolemaic bureaucracy. In Athens, when she stood by Antony at the gathering of the fleet and the armies, Cleopatra was a regal presence demanding a recognition that was owed to her on account of the history of her famous house, her own fame, her successful experience as a monarch, and her equal commitment to the dream she shared with Antony.

But Antony feared to give her this recognition, for he knew as a Roman that if he wished to govern in Rome he could not do so under the colours of an oriental despotism, which the traditions of republican Rome hated and despised. In Rome, support for a leader was freely given and freely withdrawn. A great man made an unwritten contract with the citizens, or with a portion of them, which was paid out on their part in loyalty. That loyalty was not to be taken for granted, and no one, however exalted his position or strong his army, had an automatic right to service. When Octavian tried to recruit Asinius Pollio to his cause, that upright, much-admired man replied, 'My services to Antony are too great and his kindnesses to me too well known for me to take your part in the quarrel, so I shall keep out of it and be the prize for the victor.' Octavian accepted this, for it was the old Roman way.

If Antony wished to carry his Roman followers with him, they must go through their own free choice. His best advisers were counselling him to leave Cleopatra behind at Ephesus, to try to minimize her part in the grand scheme. As long as she was seen as co-leader of the campaign, he did not dare invade Italy, for then his generals and his legions might melt away. Yet without her, he could not withstand Octavian, for she provided the sinews of his war and their imperial dream belonged to both of them. To this dilemma may be ascribed many of the military misjudgements and errors, from a soldier of Antony's experience, that have long puzzled historians. Antony delayed and delayed because he could not be seen to invade Italy. He had to force Octavian to attack him, and so bring the war out of Italy. He chose to rely on his fleet, which was as much Egyptian as Roman, because he could not put a wholehearted trust in his legions, though he had more money and more men than Octavian. Between the decline of his powers and his excessive reliance on Cleopatra, Antony was caught morose, perplexed, inconsistent. As the initiative began to leak away so too did his supporters, and he was not sure how to react. When his friend Ahenobarbus deserted he put on a nonchalant public face, scoffing that his old companion was fleeing to a mistress in Rome. In secret, despite the protests of Cleopatra, he sent the man's belongings and servants after him. But when the client-prince Iamblichus tried to desert, Antony caught him and executed him as an example.

In expectation of the spring campaign in 31 BC, Antony placed his command headquarters at Patras in Greece and formed a line of defence along the western coast of Albania and Greece. He had a large army of 19 legions as well as auxiliaries from the eastern client-kingdoms. In all, he had about 70,000 infantry and 12,000 cavalry. A few legions were left to guard his rear, thinly spread from North Africa to the Bosphorus. But his main effort, and most of Cleopatra's money, had been put into the fleet. This was another acknowledgement of his debt to Cleopatra, for Egypt had always relied on naval power while Romans much preferred to fight on land using the formidable, well-tried strength of the legions. The queen was paying for the campaign, but was it wise to let her make the military choices? Plutarch thought that the strategy shamed Antony:

> Although Antony was far stronger than Octavian on land, merely to please the queen he wished to give the victory to the fleet, even though his ships were so undermanned that his captains had to waylay and impress travellers, muleteers, farmers, and even young boys from the fields of Greece.

Coin issued in 32–31 BC depicting a Roman galley,
of a type probably in use at the Battle of Actium.

Antony's fleet of some 500 warships was as large and powerful as the ancient world had ever seen. Noting the success of Agrippa's heavily built ships against Sextus Pompeius, Cleopatra's shipwrights had gone one better than Agrippa, constructing giant floating castles with as many as ten rowers to an oar. The sides of the ships were protected by baulks of timber bound with iron, and in the prow of each was a tremendous bronze beak for ramming, for the chief tactics of a Mediterranean sea-fight were to ram, grapple and board the enemy. These vessels were hugely powerful, but also slow, awkward and almost unmanageable with poorly trained crews. Octavian's admiral Agrippa, on the contrary, having battered Sextus to defeat with brute force, now showed his naval genius by going to the other extreme. To complement his big ships, he quickly had built a large number of smaller, faster, more agile galleys based on a ship used by Adriatic pirates and known as a Liburnian. These were cheap, easy to construct and light to handle, even with inexperienced crews.

Octavian's ships [Plutarch wrote in retrospect] were not built for pomp or ostentatious show but were well-manned, fast and easy to manoeuvre.

The conduct of Antony's campaign has been a mystery to most later writers. Whereas Antony was dilatory, confused and careless, Octavian was swift, sure and decisive. Octavian acted, Antony merely reacted; and as so often the luck ran with the bold. Octavian's fleet set out from southern Italy early in 31 BC and made a number of fast, punitive strikes, both by land and sea, along the line of Antony's defences. Having turned the northern end of these defences, Octavian landed his army in Epirus and almost before Antony had drawn breath this army was on the northern headland of the Gulf of Ambracia, threatening the anchorage of Antony's fleet within the gulf. Antony came hurriedly from Patras and established a position on the southern headland, by the temple of Apollo at Actium. Both armies began to dig in and fortify; but in the rear Agrippa's raiders took Corinth and Patras, closing off the lower Greek mainland from Antony, and preventing the Egyptian supply-ships from getting through to his fleet. The two armies faced each other across the kilometre-wide mouth of the gulf, and Agrippa's pack of light galleys, like hunting dogs on a cornered stag, began a blockade of the fleet in the shelter of the gulf.

There was little concern on Antony's side at the first reverses. When Octavian landed in Epirus and took the town of Toryne, Cleopatra laughed, saying, 'Who cares if he has a ladle in his hands?', for *toryne* meant ladle in Greek. But as summer advanced the position was serious for Antony. His army had been idle for too long, camping for some time in low-lying malarial ground, and many soldiers were sick. Now there was an entrenched stalemate on land and Antony's supply-route was cut at sea. Food began to be scarce and provisions had to be dragged over the bitter country of the Greek mountains by mule and even on porters' backs. Plutarch related how his own great-grandfather had struggled under the lash towards Actium with a sack of corn on his shoulders. The besiegers, who had hoped to tie down Octavian's smaller army, were now besieged, and desertions from Antony's ranks went from a trickle to a flow. The eastern client-kings felt the advantage shift and ghosted away to an uneasy reception from Octavian. 'I like treason,' he told one of these princes, 'but I don't like traitors.' Still the haemorrhage of men continued. Amyntas of Galatia crossed over with his 2000 men, and this was the time also when Dellius and Ahenobarbus, both old companions, deserted. Time was running out but Antony could not make up his mind. His cumbersome fleet had been no use to him so far. His senior officers were telling him to abandon both his fleet and Cleopatra, to withdraw his army into Thrace or Macedonia, territories he knew well and where he had local sympathy, and to put the campaign to the test of a land battle.

> It would be absurd for Antony [wrote Plutarch, commenting on the advice that Antony received] who was as experienced a general on land as any living, to throw away the advantage of his numbers and his strength and to weaken himself by putting his soldiers in the ships. But despite these sensible words from Canidius, Cleopatra chose to fight at sea and she prevailed on Antony.

And Plutarch added darkly, though there was as yet no evidence for his statement:

The truth was that in her thoughts she was already contemplating flight, and the real purpose of her battle order was not victory but to help her escape in the event of defeat.

Cleopatra had remained by Antony's side, which was no small matter for a queen used to luxury in that bad summer of short rations, sickness and desertions in the camp. If she had cared only for her own safety, she could easily have followed the pleas of the advisers and retreated with dignity. But she was impatient for action and could not bear the thought of a strategic retreat with many long weary marches into the mountains of Thrace. She wanted a quick resolution and her Egyptian instinct was to trust to the fleet, for she could not believe that Octavian would defeat such an armada. At last, Antony's disordered judgement agreed with her and she had her way.

When he finally decided to fight at sea, Antony burned all but 60 of the Egyptian ships, then he manned the best and largest of them, those with three to ten banks of oars, and put into them 22,000 heavily armed men and 2000 archers. As he was doing this, one of his centurions, scarred and hacked in many a battle under Antony, cried out to him as he passed, 'Imperator, how is it that you trust these miserable ships? Do not my sword and my wounds speak to you? Let Egyptians and Phoenicians fight by sea, but give us land to stand on foot by foot, to conquer or to die.' Antony passed him by without a word but only made a gesture of his hand, as if wishing him to be of good heart, yet he showed no great confidence himself. For when the captains proposed to leave their sails behind, Antony ordered them to be taken aboard since they might be needed, or so he said, to run down an enemy in flight.

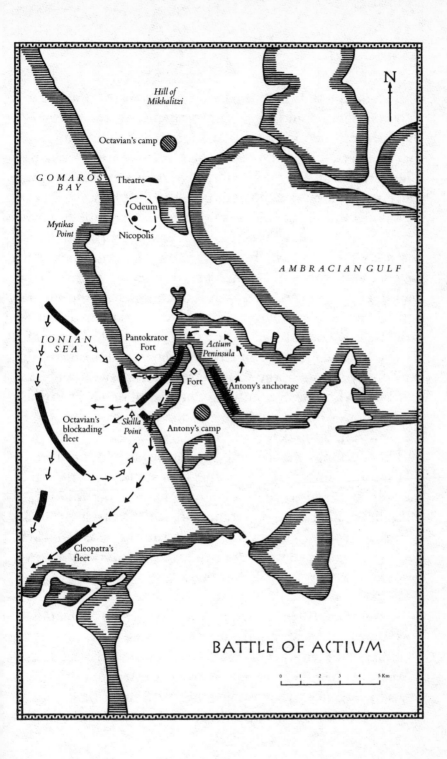

N

Hill of
Mikhalitzi

Octavian's camp

GOMAROS
BAY

Theatre

Odeum

Mytikas
Point

Nicopolis

AMBRACIAN GULF

IONIAN
SEA

Pantokrator
Fort

Actium
Peninsula

Fort

Antony's anchorage

Octavian's
blockading
fleet

Skilla
Point

Antony's camp

Cleopatra's
fleet

BATTLE OF ACTIUM

0 1 2 3 4 5 Km

To take the sails was suspicious, for the usual practice was to leave them behind when ships grappled at sea. Nor would the fighting-men have been encouraged if they had known that the war-chests had been loaded in secret on to certain of Cleopatra's transports. The most charitable explanation was that Antony, if he saw the fight going against him, would clap on all sails and break away with the treasure and the Egyptian squadron to Egypt, where he could regroup and continue the war on better terms. But these acts, however they were viewed, were those of a general who expected defeat. Octavian, however, was ready and full of confidence. On the day before the engagement he met a countryman driving a donkey. In a friendly spirit he asked the man his name and received the reply, 'My name is Eutychos, the Fortunate, and my donkey is Nikon, the Conqueror.' This answer so pleased Octavian, who saw in it nothing but a good omen, that when the battle was done he put up a bronze statue on the spot to the man and his donkey.

The morning of 2 September 31 BC began with fitful winds that subsided into a calm. Antony's fleet stood in the mouth of the gulf but made no move. Opposing but well out to sea were the galleys under Agrippa's command, with Octavian in a light Liburnian roving among them. The rowers rested on their oars, waiting to see what the wind would do. About noon a breeze arose, blowing from off the sea.

By this time [Plutarch wrote in his report of the battle] Anthony's men were impatient at the long wait, so they advanced the left wing of the fleet, thinking that the size and weight of their ships made them invincible. At once Octavian gladly responded, commanding the rowers of his right wing to back water, so as to lure the enemy from the narrows of the gulf into the open sea where his agile galleys might surround and harass the undermanned giants.

When the battle lines met Antony's heavy ships had not yet got up sufficient speed for ramming. Octavian wished to avoid these shocks, for he feared those massive armoured plates with their wicked beaks of bronze. Nor could he afford to ram amidships himself, or his own beaks would break off against the squared timbers bolted with iron. So the battle took on the character of a fight by land, or more exactly like an attack on a fortified town.

Small ships snapped at each great hull, firing arrows and darts and flaming brands, using Agrippa's device of the *harpax* (grapnels shot from a catapult) to bind fast the ships so that soldiers could board from all sides. From high turrets on poop and foredeck Antony's men fought off the swarm of attackers with fire and shot of their own. The moment was indecisive, the battle swaying back and forth.

Then Cleopatra's squadron of 60 ships was suddenly seen to hoist sail and make off from the very midst of the fight. Stationed behind the heavy ships, this squadron plunged through their line and threw them into disorder, but with straining sails before the following wind her ships set course for the Peloponnese. Now Antony, no longer a commander nor a brave man nor even one of judgement, proved the truth of that old saying, that a lover's soul dwells in the body of another, for he allowed himself to be dragged after that woman, flesh of her flesh to go wherever she would.

Unable to pull his own flagship out of the line, Antony, when he saw Cleopatra flee, transferred as quickly as he could to a smaller boat and fled after her. He came up to Cleopatra's ship and went aboard, though he neither saw her nor looked for her. Instead, he sat silent in the bows with his head in his hands. For three days he stayed there, alone and grimly silent, as the ship sped to the southern point of Greece. Weary from flight they dropped anchor at Taenarum, by Cape Matapan. Shamed past anger and too lost for recriminations at last Antony was persuaded to look on Cleopatra. They began to talk, 'and later they ate, and so went together to their sleep'.

At Actium, when the leader had fled, Antony's fleet still fought on until a half-gale rising in the afternoon broke the formation of the big ships and let the marauders in among them. At about 4 pm the fleet surrendered. The losses for such a large battle were inconsiderable, though Octavian captured some 300 warships and transports. Most of them were burnt, according to Roman practice, and the bronze beaks were used to raise a monument where Octavian's camp had stood.

The news reached Cleopatra's ship that the fleet was utterly routed, but it was said that the army still held together. When he heard this Antony sent messengers to Canidius to withdraw as quickly as possible through Macedonia into the East. As for himself, Antony said he would sail to Libya. Then he chose one of the transports of Cleopatra's squadron that carried great quantities of money and precious things, and vessels of silver and gold that belonged to the royal household. This ship he presented to his loyal friends, urging them to divide the treasure and save themselves. His friends refused with tears in their eyes, but Antony comforted them with all imaginable warmth and kindness, and still pressed them to accept his gift. Then he sent them away with a letter to

Corinth, ordering his steward there to give them safe refuge until they could make their peace with Octavian.

Canidius tried to march the army away, though it was only a half-hearted attempt and after a week the army surrendered to Octavian. Canidius himself escaped to join Antony in Egypt. Octavian's victory was overwhelmingly complete. Now, in the Roman view, Antony was beneath contempt, a soldier who had sold himself into slavery to a woman, a general fit only to take orders from a wrinkled eunuch of a debauched oriental court. Octavian, the embodiment of Roman virtue, was hailed as Imperator for the sixth, final and unassailable time. Antony, the would-be emperor of the East, was brushed from the path of history. 'The Imperator whose duty it was to punish deserters', wrote the historian Velleius, 'himself became a deserter from his own army.'

Antony sailed from Greece leaving the ruins of his ambition and reputation behind him. He landed at Paraetonium on the border of Cyrene, to wander the desert and play the malcontent. But Cleopatra put a bold face on disaster and returned to Alexandria with flags flying as if for victory. It was an astute move, well up to her usual standard for intelligence, for it allowed her to take control of the city before the disappointed and fickle populace could turn on her. She had managed to rescue a good part of her treasure in her war-chests; she had intact many of the ships of her Egyptian squadron; her country was still at peace and was productive, and she was still the royal Ptolemy, queen of the richest kingdom of the Mediterranean world. But Antony was the puzzle. Should she hand the defeated general to Rome, as the price for Egypt's safety? Or was there still enough of their joint dream left to make a new beginning based on the wealth of Egypt? She was only thirty-eight, young enough for a fresh start. But where was Antony for the grand plan, whatever it might be?

In Cyrene, with the defection of his troops to Octavian, Antony saw his cause die in North Africa as it had died in Asia Minor. He attempted suicide but was prevented by his friends. Then he returned to Alexandria; there was nowhere else to go. Wild plans were invented. The lovers would go to Spain, or better still to India, beyond the arc of the Roman sun. Cleopatra ordered ships of her Mediterranean fleet to be dragged across the narrow land isthmus to the head of the Red Sea. But Malchus of Nabataea, who had lost land to Cleopatra in Antony's settlement of 37 BC, intercepted the ships and burnt them.

Since all efforts were frustrated, nothing more seemed worthwhile. Feverish plans gave way to passivity. The eastern world was waiting for Octavian, and Egypt marked time. Antony, never very stable in his emotions, sank into despondency, but even in misery his conduct was arranged for grand effect.

> Antony abandoned the city and the company of his friends [Plutarch wrote] and built himself a little house looking towards the isle of Pharos, on a breakwater running into the sea. There, he shut himself off from human society, and asked for nothing better than to follow the example of Timon, whose fate was so like his own. Antony too, like Timon, had been wronged by the ingratitude of his friends, and for this reason he was angry with all and would trust none.

Octavian gave Antony and Cleopatra in Alexandria almost a year of grace. He needed money urgently and expected to find it in Egypt. He knew also that the fate of Antony awaited

Silver coin depicting Cleopatra, *c.* 30 BC,
the year of her death.

his decision, but he judged that Antony was a broken man
bereft of his army and he was no danger for the moment. In
the meantime, there were pressing problems in the Roman
world. Immediately after Actium, Octavian went to Athens, to
begin a provisional settlement in the lands that had owed allegiance to Antony. Athenians, realists in politics, poured on
him the honours once so freely given to Antony and Cleopatra, those who had been the New Dionysus and his Isis-
Aphrodite. The client-kings of the East, shocked by the
finality of Octavian's triumph, quickly made their peace. But
in Italy the renewed attempt to find rewards and landholdings
for the discharged veterans of the legions, and the general
impoverishment from the war, led to many disturbances.
There was a vicious mood of discontent that so often follows
the celebration of victory.

When Agrippa and Maecenas were unable to hold back this
swell of ugly feeling they sent quickly for Octavian. He sailed
at once for Brundisium, risking his life on dangerous seas that

drowned his own physician. With patient skill and much juggling of resources, with some payments now and many promises for the future, Octavian capped the well of Italian discontent. But he saw clearly that he could not make good his promises without a sudden gush of extra riches, and this was to be found nowhere else but in Egypt. In the spring of 30 BC he was back in Asia Minor, eyeing Egypt and putting together an army to march the well-trodden path from Syria to Pelusium.

Antony soon tired of his Alexandrian hermitage and crossed the Great Harbour to the better comforts of the Brucheion palace. He heard from Canidius that the remnants of his army were dispersed or had gone over to Rome, and his eastern hopes melted as quickly as the loyalty of the client-kings. Plutarch took up the story:

By this time such news no longer troubled him, for he seemed content to forego all hope and so to rid himself of care and woe. He left his solitary retreat by the sea, which he had called the Timoneum, and was welcomed by Cleopatra into the palace. And once again they set all the city to feasting and drinking, and he began to distribute lavish gifts. He caused Caesarion, son of Julius Caesar and Cleopatra, to be enrolled in the young company of ephebes, according to the usual manner, and gave the *toga virilis* of manhood, the one without the purple border, to Antyllus, his own son by Fulvia. In celebration of these events there was dancing and feasting in the city for days on end. He and Cleopatra dissolved their old riotous company of Inimitable Livers and instituted a new companionship called the Order of the Inseparable in Death, a company in no way less elegant and extravagant than the former. In this gathering all swore to end their lives together,

and until that time they charmed their days with a succession
of glorious banquets.

Whatever solace it might give to Antony, this round of
pleasure was not enough for Cleopatra. To her, Octavian was
still a great unknown and she was ready to sound out his intentions. It was said that her Egyptian subjects were eager to rise
against Rome on her behalf. But a premature uprising would
only invite disaster, and she refused to let her people act, at
least until she could make some judgement of Octavian. She
had already sent Antyllus to Octavian with a large sum of
money. Octavian kept the money but sent Antyllus back. Now
Cleopatra sent a delegation to Syria with the insignia of her
royal house, offering to surrender her crown so long as her
children might inherit the throne. This was a normal practice
in the changeable world of the client-kings, and Rome had
usually permitted it, as Octavian did with Herod, once
Antony's most ardent supporter. As for Antony, he surrendered
all rank and authority and merely asked to exist as a private citizen, if not in Alexandria then at least in Athens. Though
Antony was not even worthy of a reply, Octavian now began to
set his wits against Cleopatra. Two consummate politicians
tried to match each other in cunning and intelligence.

Octavian sent word to Cleopatra that he would grant any
request within reason so long as she would execute Antony or
banish him from Egypt. The freedman Thyrsus bore Octavian's message, for he was a shrewd man, one well able to
bring soothing, persuasive words from a young lord to a
noble lady very conscious of her powers of enchantment.
Cleopatra received this man graciously and gave him so long
an audience that Antony grew suspicious. So he had the

freedman seized and whipped and returned to Octavian, to tell him that the insolence of his messenger enraged a man whose fortunes were so low. 'If this displeases you,' said Antony, 'you have my freedman Hipparchus as your hostage. Hang him if you please, or scourge him at will, and then we shall be quits.' After this, Cleopatra took care to calm Antony with tenderness and affection. Her own birthday she kept very meanly in keeping with her misfortune, but his she celebrated with great solemnity and extravagance, so that guests who came poor to the feast went away rich.

There was spirit in Antony yet, and when the old lion was provoked he could still roar. But her meeting with Thyrsus had taught Cleopatra what she already suspected, that Antony, despite his bravado, was hurt beyond repair in mind and reputation, and Octavian was not to be trusted. She would not be a traitor to her lover but he was too wounded to help her, and Octavian would only use Antony as a means to her treasure. She began to remove the wealth of the Ptolemies, the stores of gold and silver and jewels and precious metals, into her incompleted mausoleum near the temple of Isis. In the upper part of this monument were rooms for herself and her waiting-women. The treasure was below surrounded by a great mass of combustible material ready to be set on fire. Octavian's real aim was the wealth of Egypt and the possessions of the queen. Her treasure was Cleopatra's last good bargaining counter.

In July 30 BC Octavian marched into Egypt, quickly overran Pelusium and arrived at the edge of Alexandria on the last day of the month. Summoned for one last action, Antony put on his well-worn armour and filled his lungs once more with the sharp air of conflict. Momentarily he was his old self, and in a skilful little engagement he routed the cavalry advance-guard of the Roman army. It was not enough, for the military strength of Octavian was overwhelming. Antony retired into the city as if in triumph. Smiles returned and Antony seemed something like his old tremendous figure, issuing a challenge to Octavian to meet him in single combat. Octavian retorted coolly that he had other ways to die than at the hand of such a desperado.

> With this answer Antony knew that his most honourable end was now to die in battle, and he prepared to attack next day by land and sea. At dinner that night he bade his servants treat him kindly and with all consideration, for who knew what man they might serve tomorrow, when Antony was only a dead body? Then seeing that men were weeping to hear him say so, he told his friends that he would not lead them to battle for victory or safety, but rather for the sake of an honourable death.

In the night, at about the hushed hour of midnight, men said there was a noise of music in Alexandria, and the ghostly wailing of choirs, and a hubbub of people as if revellers were leaving. The sound went along the main street of the city to the eastern Canopic gate nearest the Roman camp, and then it stopped. To the augurs, the meaning of the omen was clear. The god Dionysus, whom Antony had striven all his life to follow and to imitate, was abandoning him. It was the moment beyond self-deception and fantasy, for Antony to look upon his life and see himself for what he was. Alexandria, city of subtlety and strange understanding, gave him this hard gift at the final moment, as Cavafy, most Alexandrian of poets, so movingly described:

[169]

When at the hour of midnight
an invisible choir is suddenly heard passing
with exquisite music, with voices –
Do not lament your fortune that at last subsides,
your life's work that has failed, your schemes that have
            proved illusions.
But like a man prepared, like a brave man,
bid farewell to her, to Alexandria who is departing.
Above all, do not delude yourself, do not say it is a dream,
that your ear was mistaken.
Do not condescend to such empty hopes.
Like a man for long prepared, like a brave man,
like to a man who was worthy of such a city,
go to the window firmly,
and listen with emotion,
but not with the prayers and complaints of the coward
(Ah, supreme rapture!)
listen to the notes, to the exquisite instruments of the
            mystic choir,
and bid farewell to her, to Alexandria whom you are losing.

Next morning, Antony began calmly, making soldierly preparations for action, disposing his troops about the city, and watching the remains of his fleet put to sea. But when the sailors were beyond the harbour wall they went straight over to the enemy, and seeing this his cavalry also deserted.

Finally, when his infantry was routed, Antony withdrew into the city crying in a rage that Cleopatra had betrayed him to the very man he was fighting for her sake. In terror of his fury, the queen fled into her monument, closed the doors with locks and bars, and sent word to Antony that she was dead. Not doubting this message for a moment, Antony said to himself, 'Why do you delay? Fate has taken away your only joy and your reason for living.' Then he unarmed and laid his equipment aside, and said again, 'O Cleopatra, your loss does not hurt me, for soon I shall be with you, but it shames me that such an Imperator as I might be judged to be of less courage and nobility than a woman.'

Now Antony had a faithful servant called Eros, who had sworn to kill his master if the need arose. That time had come, and Eros drew his sword as if to strike as his master ordered. But turning aside he thrust into himself and fell at his master's feet. 'O noble Eros,' cried Antony, 'that was bravely done, to teach me to do the thing you could not accomplish for me.' Then he stabbed into his own belly, and fell bleeding upon a bed. But the wound did not kill him, and presently, as the blood flowed less, he begged his friends to make an end of him. But they ran from the room and left him in agony, till Diomedes, Cleopatra's secretary, came with orders from the queen to carry him to her monument.'

Cleopatra saw that, in her message to Antony, her cunning had out-run her prudence. And now her general, the prop of her title and state, was dying. Servants carried Antony to her monument, but even then she was afraid to open the doors, and so she lowered ropes to pull up the dying man. With many groans she and her women drew him up and laid him on a bed, covered with a dress that she tore from her body. Cleopatra beat her head and lacerated her breast and smeared herself with his blood, calling him lord and husband and emperor. Antony drank a little wine and urged her to seek her safety, but without dishonour, and told her to trust none of Octavian's men except Proculeius.

At last [wrote Plutarch] he begged her not to lament his wretched fortune, but to count him happy for the glories he had won, since he had lived as the greatest and most noble prince of the world, and now he died without dishonour, a Roman by a Roman conquered.

That same day Octavian entered Alexandria, on the first of the month later named August in his honour. In the *Fasti*, the calendar of public records in Rome, it was written that he had saved the republic from the most horrid of dangers. Since officially Cleopatra alone was the enemy, this could only mean that Rome was saved from the queen of Egypt. But before the ultimate rejoicing that queen had to be captured, and Octavian was most anxious to take her alive, to secure her treasure and her person, since he intended to show her in his triumph in Rome.

As soon as he entered the city Octavian heard of Antony's death and was shown the bloodied sword. First, he wept, for Antony was related to him by marriage and had been his colleague in the greatest affairs of the world; then he took care to read aloud from Antony's letters, to justify his own behaviour, to show how reasonable he had been at all times and how the fault lay with Antony. Then he sent Proculeius to try to tempt Cleopatra from her stronghold. But she would not open the doors and they spoke through a grating. She named her terms, that her children should be permitted to succeed her, and while Proculeius gave her soft words he also noticed the window high up, through which Antony had been drawn into the monument. He went away and made arrangements, and when another came to talk to the queen Proculeius mounted a scaling-ladder against the wall and led a posse of soldiers through the window. When Cleopatra saw that she was tricked she took a little dagger from her dress and tried to stab herself. But Romans rushed forward and pinned her arms and took her alive. Now Octavian had the treasure and the queen.

Within a few days Octavian granted an audience to Cleopatra. It was in both their interests to make a final reckoning. With her, it was a matter of life and death; but also, beyond the fate of her body, lay the fate of her Ptolemaic house and the fate of Egypt itself. These resolutions rested with Octavian, who must decide most carefully in the larger interests of Rome. The details of this meeting are not known, but many fanciful stories were embroidered around it. No doubt Cleopatra applied all her well-practised arts that had smitten and undone great men in other times. She was pathetic and forlorn, penitent and deeply wounded in mind and spirit; and when that did not work she tore at herself and raged. It was said she tried to seduce him, but in truth that was an abandoned ploy from an exhausted past dredged up here only by the poverty of literary imagination. They were not easily deceived by each other, for in depth of political understanding they were much alike. She knew that Rome intended to take it all: her person, her wealth, her right to confer the succession and her country. At this moment, death looked easy and comfortable.

For some time Cleopatra had studied death. She had made enquiries about poisons and their effects. The Order of the Inseparable in Death, her last company of friends in Alexandria, may only have been a piece of gloomy theatre, but it showed the drift of her thought. Suicide was a noble Roman way. Cato and Brutus had died thus, and now Antony had fallen by his own hand. It was not a Ptolemaic practice, but none before her had been given the Roman lesson and example that she had. Defeat braced her for death, Antony's suicide

resolved her, and Octavian's cold determination to make a dis-
grace of her and all she stood for gave her the necessary
courage. Plutarch wrote that after their meeting Octavian had
left Cleopatra 'believing that he had deceived her, but he himself was deceived'. It was a victory of a kind.

Octavian had allowed Antony an honourable funeral, and
Cleopatra begged one last chance to pour a libation to her
departed lover. Octavian, who had already made arrangements
to transport the queen and her children out of Egypt, gave
way. She went to the tomb and monument to Antony and
poured her libation and made a simple prayer out of her grief:

> O Antony, if there is any mercy or power in the gods of
> Rome, for my gods have betrayed us, do not abandon your
> wife, nor let me be led in triumph to your shame. Hide me
> and let me be buried here with you, for I know now that the
> thousand pains I have suffered in my life are as nothing
> besides the few days I have had to live without you.

On 10 August, in Antony's mausoleum, she began to make
her last preparation. The record of these events came down
from her physician Olympus into the family of Plutarch, and
the historian put them into sombre words:

> So Cleopatra mourned Antony, and crowned his urn with
> garlands and kissed it. Then she ordered a bath made ready,
> and coming from the bath she rested and was served with a
> most sumptuous meal. Now, while she was at dinner a coun-
> tryman came to her bringing a basket. When the guards
> stopped him and demanded to see what was in the basket, he
> pulled away some leaves and showed ripe figs which looked
> so good the soldiers were tempted to try them. Then

they allowed him to take the fruit to the queen. After she had dined, Cleopatra took a tablet and wrote on it for Octavian, and sealed it and sent it. Then she dismissed all but her two faithful waiting-women and closed the doors of the monument.

When Octavian received her tablet, and read her petition to be buried with Antony, he guessed at once what she intended. He thought to go himself but changed his mind and sent messengers hurrying to the queen. But death had come too fast. At the monument, the guards had seen nothing wrong, but when all the people burst through the doors they found Cleopatra dead upon a golden couch dressed in her royal robes. One of her women, who was called Iras, was dead at her feet, while the other, Charmian, tottering and scarce standing, was making straight the diadem on her mistress' brow. Seeing this, one of the guards cried angrily, 'Charmian, is this well done?' And the woman answered, 'Very well done, and fitting for a princess descended from so many kings.' Uttering these words, she fell dead by the side of the couch.

Cleopatra died by snake bite, from a cobra brought in the fig basket, though the snake was not found. The bite of the asp – the Egyptian cobra – was not painful and death from respiratory failure was quick, perhaps within thirty minutes. The famous Roman medical writer, Galen, noted that criminals in Alexandria were sometimes granted this death as a merciful execution. But for Cleopatra it was far from an execution; rather, it was an apotheosis that took the mortal parts of the goddess-queen Cleopatra and transmuted her into the Egyptian deity Isis. The asp was the *uraeus*, the snake sacred to Amon-Ra that the pharaohs carried on their insignia and wore on their headdress. Through the agency of the sacred asp the Sun God welcomed his royal and holy daughter into the pantheon of the Egyptian gods. The robes in which Cleopatra died were those of the New Isis, the robes in which she had appeared so regally on the great and public occasions of her reign. This Ptolemy, this Macedonian Greek queen, was never more Egyptian than in her death.

The death of Cleopatra, and the possession of her treasure intact, saved Octavian. When these Egyptian riches reached Rome the normal rate of interest dropped from 12 per cent to 4 per cent. Now he was able to make good the promises to his veterans, to pay for the land he had expropriated for them, and to have enough money left over for many public works besides. Some 120,000 veterans were each given 1000 sestercii, and even the people of Rome received 400 sestercii each. In this way Octavian avoided the turbulence of dissatisfaction in Italy that poverty would have forced upon him. He was at last free, and had the resources, to make final his plan for Roman greatness.

But first he had matters to clear up in Egypt. He pulled down the statues of Antony, but those of Cleopatra were left standing, for which act of grace one of her loyal friends paid a very large fee. Octavian feared no statues, but for a conqueror certain acts of revenge become a necessity. Antyllus, the eldest son and heir of Antony, was taken from asylum and killed. Nor could Caesarion be spared. In the Roman world there was room for only one Caesar. Ptolemy Caesar – Caesarion – had been sent by his mother to flee to India. But his tutor beguiled the 16-year-old with false promises of safety and led him back to Egypt where he was executed. A few others whom Octavian considered most guilty or most dangerous were killed, but these were very few in number, for Octavian was tired of bloodshed and wanted the murder to stop. The three children of Cleopatra by Antony, two boys and a girl, were taken to Rome where they walked in Octavian's triumph. Then they joined the household of Octavia, the most forgiving of wives who took to her honourable heart all the lost children of Antony, those of the spitfire Fulvia and those called by Romans the children of the harlot-queen of Egypt.

After their education in Rome, Alexander Helios and Ptolemy Philadelphus disappeared from history. Their sister Cleopatra Selene was married to Juba II of Mauretania by whom she had a son, later executed by the Emperor Caligula, and a daughter who married Antonius Felix, the governor of Judaea known to the apostle Paul. With greater irony, Antony's other children by Octavia achieved what his little Egyptian Sun and Moon had never become. They shone in the imperial firmament of Rome. One daughter was mother of Emperor Claudius and grandmother of Emperor Caligula, and the other daughter was grandmother of Emperor Nero. Thus on the death of Nero in 68 AD, when madness and folly extinguished the Julian-Claudian-Antonian clans, the ashes belonged to the house of Mark Antony not to his deadly opponent Octavian Caesar, later called Emperor Augustus.

The triumph of Octavian brought the long brutal age of civil wars to a close. The Roman revolution had run its course, taking the wheel of the state in a great cycle from republic to principate. In the time of horrors, when blood leaked like rain in the streets of Rome, good citizens prayed constantly for peace, and yearned for some authority – man or god or god-like man – to lead them out of war. The longing for peace was never more feelingly expressed than in the Fourth Eclogue of Virgil, a poem written to honour the poet's patron Asinius Pollio, the friend of Antony who did so much to bring the two sullen titans of the state to the supposed harmony of the treaty of Brundisium in 40 BC. Virgil's poem celebrated the birth of a boy who would institute a new age, the Golden Age of a new order that reconciled all difficulties and brought in the long-awaited time of universal peace and prosperity. Who was that celebrated boy? It is a mark of the ache for holy order that so many posterities have rushed to claim that child. Christians, as is well known, have seen in the Fourth Eclogue a prophecy of the birth of Christ and the new order of Christendom.

The true history seems far more modest. The most likely candidate for Virgil's bringer of peace was the expected child of Antony and Octavia. The hopes were immediately dashed, for the treaty of Brundisium did not hold, and the baby was born a girl not a boy. But the burden of expectation laid on a mysterious babe was easily transferred to a pale young Roman with a prospering future. Even in 39 BC, when the concord of Brundisium was jangling out of tune, Antony complained that his luck went into decline under Octavian's shadow.

Antony kept in his house [Plutarch wrote] an Egyptian sooth-sayer skilled in the casting of horoscopes. This man, either to please Cleopatra or because he wished Antony to know the truth, made no secret of his reading of Antony's fortune. Although glorious and brilliant by any other standard, this fortune was constantly eclipsed by Octavian, so the sooth-sayer advised Antony to stay away from his young colleague. 'Your guardian spirit', said the Egyptian, 'stands in awe of his. By itself it is proud and mettlesome, but in the presence of Octavian's spirit yours becomes daunted and submissive.' And the turn of events confirmed the soothsayer's words, for whenever the two men cast lots or threw dice, either for amusement or to make decisions, Antony was the loser.

In an age of superstition, men judged that Antony's failure was the decision of Fate. Roman hopes for a better world – a better *Roman* world – began to rest wholly on Octavian. Much hatred was directed against Cleopatra, not because Egypt was a threat to Rome, but because Cleopatra herself traduced the Roman ideal, leading a great and noble citizen into delusion and fraternal strife. 'Neither wolves nor lions', the poet Horace wrote angrily, 'are so fiercely blind that they scratch and tear at their own kind. Is it a madness, or the result of sin?' If Antony had sinned, he was drawn into it by Cleopatra. Virgil pictured Antony facing Octavian at the battle of Actium, deceived by the wealth of the orient gathered from 'the nations of the Dawn', and followed most shamefully by 'an Egyptian wife'.

More and more, Octavian was seen as the necessary saviour. He was 'giver of fruits, ruler of seasons, god of the boundless seas'. In the *Aeneid*, that encomium for Rome and her divine mission to civilize all the known world, Virgil placed the burden of this task squarely on Octavian's slim shoulders:

> This is the man you have been promised, Augustus Caesar, dear offspring of a god, who will take the Golden Age, founded in Latium, through all those lands where Saturn reigned of old and extend his empire to the Indian shores.

To stand in the way of this beneficence was an abominable evil, and for this reason if no other Cleopatra and all her works must be expunged from the face of the world. The time of universal harmony was near. Once, when Octavian's mother was pregnant with her son, she had fallen asleep in the temple of Apollo, and she had dreamed that the god himself was

Coin depicting the triumphant Emperor Augustus in a chariot
over an arch, issued in Asia Minor in 29–27 BC.

struggling from her womb. Not even Cleopatra, with all her
Egyptian arts, could stand against the light of Apollo. Now
she was gone, and the god's time had come.

In January 27 BC, Octavian enacted his great fiction.
Already the undisputed ruler of the Roman world, in a gesture
of magnificent abasement he handed his authority back to the
senate and people of Rome. In gratitude Romans returned to
him all that his heart desired. Laurel decked his doorposts,
and the hero's wreath of oak leaves was paced above the portal
to signify that he had preserved the lives of his fellow citizens.
In the senate house a golden shield was inscribed for him with
the words 'Valour, Clemency, Justice, Piety'. And lastly he was
honoured with the title Augustus, meaning (as the historian
Dio Cassius said) 'someone who was more than human'. He
was pre-eminently *princeps civitatis* – the First Citizen. In
return for peace and security Rome had tossed away forever
its republican freedom and embarked on the new adventure of
the Principate, the long years of empire, guided and directed

[180]

by the voice of one man alone: he who had been Octavian but was now Augustus Caesar, the Emperor of Rome.

The success of the Principate, the Golden Age devised by Augustus, depended crucially on the economic strength of Egypt. In so far as Cleopatra had fostered and protected Egyptian production and trade she helped to secure the future of the Roman empire. For within a few years of Cleopatra's death, when the inevitable neglect from the time of war had been put right, Egypt began to send Rome some five million bushels of grain a year, which was about a third of the total requirement. And to add to this agricultural wealth, there were large profits that resulted from the geographical position of Egypt, at the hub of the trade routes both by land and sea, between the Mediterranean and the further reaches of Africa and India. Historically, the riches of Egypt had seemed inexhaustible, and so they appeared to Augustus. He never let Egypt out of his own hands. Though in name a province like any other in the empire, Egypt remained in fact the personal estate of the emperor. No Roman senator could visit the land

Coin depicting a crocodile and the words
'Egypt captured', issued in 28 BC.

[181]

without the permission of Augustus, and he governed this imperial fief through his own nominee, a prefect drawn from the modest ranks of the *equites* completely devoted to the emperor.

The battle of Actium had all the appearance of the last contest. Old Egypt, the 4000-year-old conservative mystery that belonged to the pharaohs, peopled by a docile peasantry in awe of changeable gods with heads of cow or dog or falcon, had fallen to the vigorous new gods of the Capitol, more rational beings who expressed the simple aspirations of an expanding, confident, warlike state. Apollo, in particular, had let in the light, and Augustus was his faithful servant.

> Yours, my Roman, is the gift of government [wrote Virgil, chief cheerleader of the new polity] that is your task: to impose upon the nations the code of peace; to be merciful to the conquered, and utterly to crush the stubborn.

But the retrospect of history reveals stranger patterns and anomalies. Not only had old Egypt survived through its economic strength, becoming the indispensable breadbasket of the Roman world, but also the long continuous Egyptian tradition, shading almost imperceptibly from pharaonic into Hellenistic, infiltrated Roman thought, even in the boasted realm of government. Augustus owed more to Cleopatra than he could ever have admitted. She was the last great systematizer and enforcer of Ptolemaic policy. In this she was the true inheritor to Ptolemy Soter, and through him to his master Alexander the Great. Augustus ardently desired a time of universal goodwill, a peaceful community of mankind under the law. But this, almost exactly, was the Hellenistic concept of *homonoia* – community of outlook and interest –

that Cleopatra strove to make general within her territories. One of the best scholars of this period set out the ideal of the Hellenistic states in this way:

> They strove, often unsuccessfully, to restore *homonoia*, concord, in the city. Taken in bulk, the surviving decrees are a paean in praise of *homonoia*. Every form of authority – kings, envoys, governors, generals – was perpetually urging the people to live in concord; the most praised women of the time, a Phila or an Apollonis, were those who tried to promote it. Homonoia herself was worshipped as a goddess at Iasos and Priene, and in Ptolemaic Thera, Artemidoros set up an altar to her 'for the city'. She was one of the great conceptions of the Hellenistic age, but she remained a pious aspiration only. Not until Rome had crushed all internal feuds was concord achieved; then, in the Imperial period, cities freely celebrated Homonoia on their coinage, and she was frequently worshipped when all meaning in her worship had for Greeks passed away.

This was a gift from old thought to raw power. And Augustus brought about his imperial concord first by the exercise of raw power, a universal subjugation under the Roman sword, but then by a wholesale borrowing from his last and most dangerous adversary, Cleopatra. For Augustus slowly built up a bureaucracy that owed far more to the rigorously centralized Ptolemaic model than to the free play of the old democratic Roman institutions. He also established for himself a form of kingship (in all but name) that was every bit as regal, peremptory and authoritarian as the Ptolemaic rule of Cleopatra. It was no wonder that Egypt so easily assimilated Augustus into the line of the pharaohs, for he was a pharaoh, not only in

Egypt but under another designation in the empire as well. He, like the pharaohs and the Ptolemies, was a god-king; and though Augustus himself was too wise to be seduced by divinity, his unbalanced successors were thoroughly deluded by the aroma of incense. Emperor Gaius, known as Caligula, thought he could make a Ptolemaic marriage with his sister, and Nero wished to create like a god and annihilate like one too.

Was this the triumph of Asia over Rome, which more than two centuries of Sibylline oracular verse had prophesied? Was Cleopatra the hidden instrument for that great work? No one can know for sure what Cleopatra herself thought. History, which judges from her acts, has found this to say of her:

We only know the great prophecy of that nameless Greek, who foretold that after she had cast Rome down from heaven to earth she would then raise her up again from earth to heaven, and inaugurate a golden age in which Asia and Europe should alike share, when war and every other evil thing should quit the earth, and the long feud of East and West should end forever in their reconciliation and in the reign of justice and love. It was surely no unworthy cause that could give birth to such a vision, or make men, even one man, see in Cleopatra the ruler who should carry out Alexander's dream of human brotherhood. We know what Augustus was to do; but if Antony was to be Roman Emperor, and Cleopatra was to be the instrument of Alexander's idea of the reconciliation of East and West, can we say that the ultimate ideals of the two sides were so very far apart after all?

What were far apart were the actual possibilities. Past history had shown that if such ideals were ever to be realized, however imperfectly, it could only be done from the West, by a Roman through Romans; no one, Roman or Macedonian, could have done it from or through the East, for he could never have carried Rome with him. In that sense, but perhaps in that sense alone, the common verdict is just, that it was well for the world that Octavian conquered.

The most brilliant of all Cleopatra's deep political perceptions was the clear understanding that Egypt could never be saved from Rome except by a Roman. Where she faltered was in her failure to go further and see that no Roman, not even Julius Caesar or Antony, could do this for her country so long as she herself was in his train. And always it was her country, or rather her Ptolemaic dynasty which she equated with her country, that she had foremost in mind. She had many chances to become a subservient pander to Roman plans, chances that would have preserved her life and living, but to her Egypt was unthinkable if it were not Ptolemaic Egypt, and she served her dynasty to the bitter end.

Rome never feared Egypt, whose soldiers raised hardly a sneer on the lips of the legionaries. But Romans did fear Cleopatra. And since history is generally written from the point of view of the victors, it is very difficult to arrive at a just estimate of her. Looking back after a century on the events of this time, Tacitus, greatest of Roman historians, wrote truly:

> Augustus, *princeps senatus*, took under his command a commonwealth exhausted by civil dissensions. There was no lack of authors competent to write the history of his times, but they were deterred by the prevailing atmosphere of flattery.

Avoiding the shoals of prejudice and malice we can make an assessment, from inscriptions, public records and the documents of her administration, of what Cleopatra hoped to achieve and how she went about it. Better, perhaps, we can find her embedded in the lasting memory of mankind. In Egypt, for many years after her death, she was simply 'the queen' who needed no other indication. It was said that many hated her, which was no doubt true at various times in her 21-year reign in mutable and violent Alexandria. But in her last extremity, with Romans at the gate, her Egyptian subjects offered to rise up against Rome on her behalf, though she forbade them, and as soon as she was gone Upper Egypt did revolt against Octavian. Her subject Archibius, an Alexandrian, ransomed her statues for 2000 talents, so that they would survive in her city as Antony's had not. Two centuries later she was still a legend in Alexandria, where the writer Apion saluted her memory. Indeed, many wonders of the past were wrongly attributed to her, so strong was the aura of her memory. It was said that she had built the Brucheion palace, and the Heptastadion dividing the two harbours, and even the Pharos lighthouse, the grandest practical construction of the ancient world, worthy of the land that made the pyramids. It was said, too, that she could transmute base metals into gold, though it was Egypt and the Nile that poured gold drop by drop into her Alexandrian treasury. Six hundred years after her death she was still not forgotten. A Coptic bishop, John of Nikiu, called her 'the most illustrious and wise among women', praising her for deeds beyond any accomplished by her forebears, or she was 'in courage and strength great in herself, and in her achievement'. Even in most hostile Rome the statue raised to her by Julius Caesar in the temple of Venus Genetrix was still in place three hundred years later.

Of those who came before her, only Alexander the Great outshone her, but in her breadth of vision and capacity to rule she borrowed some of his radiance. Even her notorious sexuality was worthy of a queen, beguiling men according to her will, an instrument loaned by her femininity to her state-craft, on a par with her intelligence, her regality, her determination and ruthlessness, and her occasional cruelty.

Since such a person exists in the imagination as much as she lived in the world of men and women, it is fitting that the last words should come from poets. Horace, Roman enough to damn her ambition and her meddling, could not but help acknowledge her greatness. At her death, he wrote:

> Yet in this Female Portent there remains
> – O great of soul – no horror of the sword.
> She scorns to live unqueenly; and she deigns
> No citizen life, ruled by an alien lord.
> Calmly she regards her palace funeral pyre
> And bids the asp perform her last desire,
> Unmoved, too proud to bear a Roman's chains.

And Shakespeare, putting into words the wonder not of a contemporary Roman but of all time, wrote simply and without any rhetorical flourish:

> She shall be buried by her Antony.
> No grave upon the earth shall clip in it
> A pair so famous.

ACKNOWLEDGEMENTS

CHAPTER 7

p. 170 'The God Abandons Antony': poem by C. P. Cavafy, trans. by George Valassopoulos.

p. 183 W. W. Tarn and J. G. Griffith, *Hellenistic Civilization* (1952), p. 90f.

pp. 184–5 W. W. Tarn, *Cambridge Ancient History*, vol. 10, pp. 82–3.

The publishers are grateful to the following for permission to reproduce photographs:

COLOUR PLATES

AKG Photo: Plates 9, 13 (Vatican Museums, Rome), 14 *above* (Kettaneh College, New York), 14 *below* (Louvre, Paris); The Ancient Art and Architecture Collection Ltd: Plates 1 *top left and right, centre left and right*, 2 *above*, 12 *above*; The Bridgeman Art Library/ Christie's London: Plates 6, 8 (Museo e Gallerie Nazionali di Capodimonte, Naples); Christie's Images: Plates 7 *above*, 15; Mary Evans Picture Library: Plate 7 *below*; Sonia Halliday Photographs: Plate 10 *below*; Robert Harding Picture Library (Photo Gavin Hellier): Plate 2 *below*; Michael Holford: Plates 4 and 5; Jonathan Lewis: Plate 11; Peter Sanders Photography: Plate 1 *below*; Geoff Thompson: Plate 10 *above*; National Museum of Wales: Plate 16; Bruce Wills: Plate 12 *below*.

BLACK AND WHITE ILLUSTRATIONS

The Bridgeman Art Library: page 39; Mansell/Time Inc.: pages 10, 29.

INDEX

Page numbers in *italics* indicate
textual illustrations

INDEX